Boundary Waters

Canoe Camping
With Style

Boundary Waters

Canoe Camping With Style

By
Cliff Jacobson

Illustrated By
Cliff Moen

ICS Books, Inc.
Merrillville, Indiana

Published by:
ICS BOOKS, Inc.
1370 E. 86th Place
Merrillville, IN 46410
800-541-7323

recycled paper

All ICS titles are printed on 50% recycled paper from pre-consumer waste. All sheets are processed without using acid.

LIBRARY OF CONGRESS CATALOGING-IN-PUBLICATION DATA

Jacobson, Cliff.
    Boundary waters: canoe camping with style / Cliff Jacobson.
        p.   cm.
    ISBN 1-57034-007-2:
    1. Canoes and canoeing – Minnesota – Boundary Waters Canoe Area.
2. Camping – Minnesota – Boundary Waters Canoe Area. 3. Boundary Waters Canoe Area (Minn.) – Description and travel. I. Title.
GV790.J32 1995
796.54'09776'7--dc20   94-40534
                                                                         CIP

Dedication

To John Baumann

A kind and gentle man
whose dreams took him beyond the beaten path.

Contents

CHAPTERS

8. THE RIGHT STUFF!

Packsacks, tents, tarps, cookware, personal clothing and footware, and edged tools. Bargain basement camping items everyone can afford. Clothing for children and teenagers. Modern comfort aids; tumplines and hip belts; how to pack your gear and the canoe; fishing gear you don't need.

Gourmet meals without glass bottles or cans to pollute the environment. Meal management tricks and food preparation tips. Grocery store alternatives to expensive freeze-dried foods. How to dehydrate and vacuum seal foods. Assemble your own cook-set.

Tricks for making a campfire in rain, and on heavily used campsites where "all the good wood has been picked over." Banking the fire in prolonged rain. How to stormproof your camp and protect your food from bears, birds and pesky mice. Smoothing the way for babies and children.

Unique tips for living comfortably with mosquitoes, black flies and no-seeums.

Swimming do's and don'ts, lightning, wind and "widow-makers"; when your canoe becomes a kite, safety with edged tools, water quality and water treatment procedures, medicine for the Boundary Waters, treatments for common ailments; signals---when you need to bring the airplane down!

Arise with the sun, prepare a steaming breakfast, pack up and start the day in 90 minutes. Cruise silently in the chill of morning fog and pause for lunch on a lichen-splashed outcrop. Experience a sudden squall and run some brawny waves. Wait out a storm beneath your propped-up, overturned canoe, then portage through dense swamp in a warm, determined drizzle. Come upon a moose feeding quietly among the lily pads and catch a mess of fish for supper. Camp on a secluded point on a dead-end lake. Experience the fire glow of a red-setting sun and the peacefulness of a perfect day in the BWCA.

Equipment check list

Important Addresses

Seven day menu

The Wilderness Meal--A non-intimidating backcountry ethics learning activity that's designed to teach low impact camping procedures to those who will experience their first Boundary Waters adventure--ideal for schools, scouts, summer camps and nature centers.

McKenzie map index

Two favorite strokes for the stern paddler

A Note
to the Reader

What? Another book on canoeing the Boundary Waters? That was my reaction when friends prodded me to write this book. However, as my thoughts began to meld, I realized that my background as both a Boundary Waters guide and Canadian river expedition trip leader could shed new light on traditional ways.

For example, lightweight camping equipment has simplified the BWCA experience, though some traditional products like Duluth packs, Minnesota style canoe yokes, wool shirts and L.L. Bean boots, continue to defy the competition.

Thankfully, campfires are still permitted in the Boundary Waters, though most modern voyageurs prefer to cook on single burner trail stoves. However, special techniques are required to prevent thick soups and cereals from burning in the intense heat of a gasoline stove. I'll share these "expedition tricks" with you in chapter 9, along with my most popular recipes, like "pita pizza" and "garlic/cheese pita melts," "dehydrated hamburger/mushroom/vegetable soup" and steamed "cinnamon-sugar tortillas." You'll also learn how to use pot insulators and cozies to save stove fuel and keep foods hot.

In chapters 2 and 4, you'll discover that you don't have to make tough portages to get away from the crowd! In chapter 10, there are serious skills for maintaining command when the weather turns sour. Chapter 12 details safety concerns and hazards which are unique to this land of proud granite. If you'll be tripping in June when the insects are bad, you may want to avoid dark blue clothing and construct the"Susie bug net," described in chapter 11. If you're canoeing with kids, you'll want to read the field-proven advice in chapter 8.

In time, you may grow to relish the challenge that comes with rain, wind, waves and unfamiliar routes. As you gain experience, you'll come to realize that knowledge, not expensive gear is what's most needed to make an enjoyable trip through the Boundary Waters.

Most of all, I hope you'll gain an appreciation for the fragile nature of the BWCA, and a deep respect for the men and women who have fought—and continue to fight—to preserve its wild heritage. New federal regulations (you'll read all about them in chapter 5) plus a better visitor distribution program ensure that the wildness of this region will remain intact for future generations to enjoy.

Cliff Jacobson

Preface

The Boundary Waters Canoe Area (BWCA) is a hauntingly beautiful place—a million acres of glaciated bedrock covered with birch and pine forests, laced with over a thousand sparkling lakes. Rivers and streams, or portage trails through the woods, connect these lakes along and just south of the international border between Minnesota and Ontario. Cliffs plunge deep into lakes here, rivers tumble over waterfalls and through rapids, and loons yodel their eerie calls across moonlit lakes.

An original unit of the National Wilderness Preservation System, the BWCA is the largest wilderness east of the Rockies and north of Florida's Everglades. This unique region contains the largest block of virgin forest in the eastern U.S., and provides home to a host of native wild species like moose, otter, bald eagles and the rare eastern timber wolf.

The BWCA is also an integral part of an international wilderness complex known as the Quetico-Superior Ecosystem. This broader region includes Ontario's 1.2 million acre Quetico Provincial Park, the 219,000 acre Voyageurs National Park just west of the Boundary Waters, and other key lands. Altogether, the Quetico-Superior Ecosystem is an internationally significant treasure of some 2.5 million acres!

The Boundary waters has not always enjoyed wilderness protection. We are the recipients of a storied legacy which began in the early part of this century. Through the efforts of wilderness advocates like Sigurd Olson, Ernest Oberholtzer, Bob Marshall, Bud Heinselman and thousands of others, the BWCA remains free from resource and recreational development. But preserving the wildness of this wilderness requires unrelenting vigilance.

Surprisingly, the world's most famous canoe country is at risk by those of us who come to explore its waterways and seek its charms. Because of its beauty and allure, the Boundary Waters is the most heavily visited wilderness in the nation. An estimated 200,000 people annually accumulate 1.5 million "recreation visitor days" of use in the BWCA. Unless we ensure that adequate protections are in place, we threaten to love the area to death, damaging campsites and destroying the very solitude and silence we seek.

All of us who visit the canoe country must remember that the wilderness was there first, that the area and its wildlife have immense "biocentric" values beyond just recreation. We must learn how to leave no trace of our passing, and to practice minimum impact camping techniques. We must remain alert for practices that would threaten the wildness of the Boundary Waters and willingly embrace environmental organizations which press for protective policies. If we care enough about the Boundary Waters we can pass on a priceless legacy of protected wilderness to our heirs.

Kevin Proescholdt
Director, *Friends of the Boundary Waters Wilderness*

CHAPTER ONE

A Wilderness in Turmoil

by David Backes

*There's something about this rugged land
that fills people with peace and makes them ready to do battle!*

David Backes holds a PhD in environmental communication from the University of Wisconsin-Madison, and is a professor in the Department of Mass Communication at UW-Milwaukee. He fell in love with the Boundary Waters in 1963, when his family first visited the area. Mr. Backes has authored three powerful books which I commend to your attention. *Canoe Country: An Embattled Wilderness* (NorthWord Press, 1991) is a lively history of the Boundary Waters that has received international praise. *The Wilderness Companion* (NorthWord Press, 1992), is a thought-provoking collection of memorable quotes from a variety of respected sources. Soon to be published is *A Wilderness Within:* The life story of wilderness giant, Sigurd F. Olson.

(C.J.)

In June 1921, a twenty-two-year-old Nashwauk, Minnesota high school teacher made his first canoe trip into the Boundary Waters, and recorded observations in a pocket-sized notebook. "This is beautiful," he wrote one afternoon while windbound on a rocky island in Sea Gull Lake. "Everything is as God made it, untouched by man. My dreams have come true. I've seen real wild country and have not been disappointed."

He almost died before the trip began, barely avoiding a plunge over a waterfall, and his notebook describes mosquito-ridden nights, painful portaging and two times when his group was lost for hours, but Sigurd Olson was hooked. Within two years he moved to Ely, Minnesota, right at the edge of the Boundary Waters, and began developing his long relationship with wilderness that eventually bore fruit in widely read books of nature essays and in his work as a leader in the struggle to save the last great remnants of North American wilderness. Through it all, he fought longest and hardest to make it possible for future generations to experience genuine wildness in the Boundary Waters he had loved since 1921.

While few achieve the kind of recognition enjoyed by a Sigurd Olson, many have followed the same basic pattern: The canoe country steals their hearts, and eventually their time.

Call it a paradox. There's something about this rugged land that fills people with peace and makes them ready to do battle.

And there have been plenty of battles over the Boundary Waters, involving more court hearings and pieces of legislation than probably any other wilderness area in North America. I don't know of another wilderness, for example, that has been raided by the FBI.

You haven't heard that story? It happened in 1953, four years after President Harry Truman had signed a precedent-setting executive order forbidding airplanes from flying into the Boundary Waters. The owners of three resorts on Crooked Lake and Lac la Croix had challenged the order in federal court and lost. They planned on appealing to the U.S. Supreme Court (the court ultimately refused to hear the case), but meanwhile they defied a federal appeals court injunction and continued to fly in up to two hundred people a day.

On June 30, 1953, three FBI agents and two U.S. marshals joined forest rangers and game wardens in Ely and planned the operation. On July 2 the U.S. marshalls flew to the resorts, seized the planes, arrested the pilots, and handed subpoenas to the resort owners. Over the next several days Forest Service officials flew stranded resort guests back to Ely, where they were questioned by the FBI agents and had their fishing licenses checked by the game wardens. The New York Times ran stories three days in a row, with such titles as "Campers Stranded as U.S. Seizes Planes Violating Ban in Minnesota," and "Two Hundred in Woods Face Rough Trip Home."

It sounds funny now, but it was deadly earnest at the time. The airplane controversy was among the most bitter in the canoe country's history. In Ely it turned some families inside out. Neighbors wouldn't speak to each other. People who attended the same church would turn away from each other.

The city's establishment was decidedly pro-airplane, so it was especially tough for those who favored banning planes from the wilderness. The Ely Miner published flagrant lies about airplane opponents. Sigurd Olson, for example, returned from a canoe trip in August 1948 to find himself accused of owning stock in timber companies, and trying to ban airplanes so the loggers could clearcut the interior portions of the wilderness without being seen. In the charged atmosphere people actually believed it.

Another Miner story, equally false, sparked death threats against Frank Hubachek, a leading proponent of the airplane ban. Then there was the owner of Ely's radio station, who sold the station shortly after broadcasting a story about fishermen illegally flying fish out of the wilderness; he said he couldn't take the threats anymore. And a small bomb was detonated in the backyard of Bill Rom, an outfitter who favored the ban.

I often think of the courage of those people in Ely and Winton and Tower and other northeastern Minnesota communities who stood up for their belief in preserving the wilderness canoe country despite the harassment they knew they would endure. Sigurd Olson was not the only one who was told he would lose his job if he kept up his wilderness activism, he's just the best known. And eventually his fame protected him from most kinds of abuse, at least if you don't count his being hanged in effigy at the age of 78.

At times the same kind of courage has been required of canoe country defenders outside of northeastern Minnesota. I think especially of a battle against waterpower development in the late 1920s and early 1930s. Edward W. Backus, one of the last of the timber barons, wanted to build a series of storage dams, and eight of them were to be built smack in the middle of the canoe country. The dams would have generated twenty thousand horsepower for his power dams between Rainy Lake and Lake Winnipeg. They also would have raised lake levels as high as eighty feet in places, flooding thousands of miles of shoreline. Basswood Falls, Curtain Falls, Rebecca and Birch falls would have been wiped out. Lac la Croix would have lost nearly all of its three hundred islands.

A group of brave men, however, formed an organization called the Quetico-Superior Council to fight Backus. Rallying behind a proposal for an international wilderness reserve that was drafted by an energetic and visionary man named Ernest Oberholtzer, the Council put Backus on the defensive and ultimately outlasted him. But it wasn't easy on the activists, many of them from Minneapolis and Chicago. Backus pulled out all the stops, getting banks to call back notes of those who opposed his plan, and using contacts to put pressure on them in the workplace.

Fighting Boundary Waters battles hasn't always required heroism, however. Every fight has had its heroes, but every fight has depended in the end on the just plain hard work of average people who love the wilderness. Rarely do they get any publicity, just the satisfaction of contributing to a cause in which they deeply believe.

Frank Robertson, of Minnesota's Mesabi Range country, was the epitome of these foot soldiers. Not especially articulate, not one to give lengthy speeches or write articles or lobby legislators, he played a key role in the fight to ban airplanes from the wilderness. He took a documentary film about the issue from town to town all over northeastern Minnesota, showing it to any civic group that would let him in: Rotary clubs, garden clubs, American Legions, church groups, chambers of commerce. Over the course of a couple of years worth of weekends and weekday evenings he showed the film more than eight hundred times, wearing out his first copy after five hundred showings.

Because of Frank Robertson's efforts more than seventy-five organizations passed resolutions in favor of the airplane ban. This provided empirical evidence to counter the claims of airplane supporters that local opinion was solidly behind them, and made it easier for the newly elected Senator Hubert Humphrey and for Representative John Blatnik to risk siding with the preservationists. If they had opposed the ban, President Truman would not have signed the executive order.

There have been too many other battles to describe in this short space -- battles over logging and outboard motors and snowmobiles, for example -- but they always have addressed the same basic question: What kind of place should the Boundary Waters be? If it is meant to provide people not just with clean air, physical adventure, and mouth-watering walleyed pike, but also with experiences of solitude and silence and a sense of kinship with the natural world from which they come, then the answer is clear: This is no place for logging or motors, and the number of visitors must carefully be managed.

If this is your answer, be prepared to defend it, for to carry out such convictions inevitably means hurting the interests of a number of other people, most of whom live near the canoe country. It's easy to stereotype resort owners and loggers as greedy, and to portray other area residents who oppose further restrictions as narrow-minded and selfish, but in fact they're just like everyone else. They've got children to feed and clothe, mortgages to pay, health insurance to purchase, and retirement savings to worry about. The difference is that they live next to this beautiful wilderness, and either depend on the canoe country for their living or for their primary recreation. Compared to people living in large cities, they have fewer options to fall back upon when their livelihood is threatened.

Also, realize that northeastern Minnesotans have never enjoyed much control over their economy. The big logging companies came and went, and, later, so did most of the mining companies. Local people never controlled these companies; their jobs were at the whims of people who lived far away. Tourism has been the most significant locally-controlled industry this part of the state has ever had; no wonder area residents often react heatedly to proposed wilderness regulations.

Those of us who want to keep the Boundary Waters wild have a double task, then: To be vigilant for threats to the tangible and intangible qualities that make the canoe country precious, and to do so in a way that does not place an unjust burden on the people who live nearby. Anything that we can do to promote a healthy and environmentally sound local economy will reap wilderness benefits.

Finding some sort of common ground, or at least building mutual respect, between non-local preservationists and area residents will become increasingly important over the next half century, because the Great Lakes region is likely to improve its industrial base. The West is running out of water, but the Midwest has it in abundance. A large increase in the region's population will certainly mean a large increase in potential visitors to the Boundary Waters. There quite likely will be pressure to relax the daily limits on the number of people who can enter the wilderness. Preservationists will find it easier to defend visitor restrictions if they can work with area residents to attract tourist traffic to the lakes and woods outside of the wilderness.

Yes, there will be battles ahead. That is a given. But as long as there are people who not only love the wilderness but are willing to give of themselves to defend it, there is hope. The next time you visit the Boundary Waters, remember this. And when you find yourself at peace some evening as the sun casts its last quivering rays over the water and a loon gives out a long, mournful cry -- when it finally hits you just how quiet it is --remember how that solitude and silence was bought for you by the sweat and dedication of hundreds of people over many years. Remember them. Enjoy the spirit of the wild. And vow to defend it.

CHAPTER TWO

Planning & Pacing Your Canoe Trip

I grew up in southern Indiana where a two-acre farm pond qualifies as a lake. So imagine my chagrin when I got my first view of the Boundary Waters from a sandy rise above Saganaga lake. Ten miles long and half as wide, Saganaga had hundreds of islands, bays and channels to confuse the route our Grand Marais outfitter had outlined on our map. And beyond the wind-protected shoreline there were whitecaps, big ones! I searched the lake for sign of a canoe. There was none.

My partner and I exchanged worried glances then burst out laughing. Back home in Indiana we were pros; here in Minnesota we were Cheechakos in a foreign land. Canoe this heaving lake today? No way!

After a short discussion, we decided to reverse our proposed route and begin our trip on nearby Seagull Lake. Seagull was about half the size of Saganaga and it had more islands to break the wind. We figured that once we reached Miles island, we could follow the lee shore all the way to the first portage.

We encountered breaking waves as soon as we cleared the channel and headed west onto the big lake. Eyes glued to our maps, we threaded our way through a maze of wind-protected islands. Thirty minutes later, we identified the small rock-walled harbor of Miles Island, where we paused to reflect on the fate of other canoeists who might not be so proficient in map and compass work.

"I'll bet a lot of people spend a lot of time paddling around wondering where they're at," mused my friend John Orr.

No sooner had he got the words out when three canoes paddled slowly towards us. When they were within hailing distance, a man called out, "You guys know where we are?"

"Miles Island," I yelled proudly. The man waved his thanks and the canoes went on their way.

Contrary to popular belief, experienced canoeists *do* get lost in the Boundary Waters, though usually not for very long. Veteran paddlers know that new routes breed new challenges. Probing an unfamiliar stream to its hidden source, finding an obscure portage or bay is all part of the Boundary Waters experience. Wondering what's around the next bend adds adventure to what might otherwise be a bland vacation.

If you want to see the Boundary Waters in a fresh new light on every trip you take, you must accept the uneasiness (call it mild fear, if you will) that often accompanies breaking new ground. However, until you've earned your wings, you'll want to keep challenges small, short and manageable. It takes years to develop good judgment and proficient outdoor skills. You can't rush time.

Let's put things into perspective with this scenario:

Four of you—all good friends—are planning a canoe trip into the Boundary Waters. Figure on seven days of mid-summer fun and adventure. The crew wants an interesting and diverse route—one with beaver ponds, streams, small rapids, marginally big lakes and picturesque water falls. A few tough portages are okay, as long as they're not too long. Relative isolation is a must. Paddling days should be short—five hours at most, and there should be at least one layover day, on which everyone can just hang around. Here's how to realize your dream:

FIRST, PICK YOUR TRAVEL AREA

Write the U.S. Forest Service, P.O. Box 338, Duluth, MN 55801 (phone 218-720-5324) and request their free pamphlet, *Welcome To The Superior National Forest*. This handy brochure contains an abbreviated map and list of 86 BWCA entry points (figure 2-1), permit and fee information, rules and regulations, and the names and addresses of Forest Service Ranger stations and tourist associations which service the Boundary Waters. Appendix 2 contains the most important U.S. and Canadian addresses.

For planning purposes, the Boundary Waters can be broken into four zones, each of which presents different challenges.

The northwestern edge of the BWCA (*Cook Area*) is characterized by huge lakes like Trout, Crane and Vermillion. The Namakan River, which originates at sprawling Lac la Croix and terminates on the edge of Voyageur's National Park, is a classic whitewater route for experienced paddlers who like big rapids. Of course, there are more intimate routes, like the Nina Moose and Little Indian Sioux Rivers, but basically this is big lake country—better suited to motor boats than canoes. On the whole, beginners will find better canoeing farther east.

Ely: Once a strong mining town, Ely now caters largely to the canoeing crowd. Attractions include the International Wolf Center, Vermillion Interpretive and History Museum (it's great!) and the world renown Soudan underground mine. A number of commercial outfitters offer state-of-the art gear at very reasonable prices.

The area around Ely has routes for every skill level. The more popular lakes—Moose, Basswood, Snowbank, Lakes One, Two, Three and Four—are fairly large and complex, and are very heavily traveled. There are smaller waters, though accessing them often means starting your trip on big water and/or making some tough portages. Exceptions include the wind-sheltered Kawishiwi and Isabella Rivers which lie off highway 1.

Tofte/Isabella: Twenty-five miles southwest of Grand Marais, on highway 61, is the rustic Tofte Ranger station which stands sentry to the famed Sawbill Trail.

Most Sawbill area lakes are small and easy-to-navigate. Portages are well maintained, reasonably short and easy to find. And the scenery is among the best in the Boundary Waters. For example, Brule and Cherokee Lakes are renown for their high cliffs, rugged shorelines and beautiful overlooks. Cherokee Creek, which is maintained by a large beaver colony, silently winds through a mile of prime moose habitat.

Grand Marais is my favorite jumping off place. Part of the allure is the town itself, which overlooks Lake Superior. There's a harbor, lighthouse and several tourist shops and restaurants, plus a renovated turn-of-the-century hotel (the East Bay). Joyne's general store contains everything from socks and popcorn to long underwear and frying pans. The Superior North Shore drive is one of the most beautiful in the world.

The Gunflint trail heads north out of Grand Marais and accesses some of the most diverse canoe country in the Boundary Waters. In chapter 4, I've outlined some of my favorite routes which originate in

Figure 2-1

this area. Ham, Round, Bearskin, Gunflint, Poplar and Seagull Lakes are jump-off points to hundreds of routes which are ideal for those who are just getting their sea legs. Appendix 5 (the McKenzie map index) provides an overview of this region.

If you want to get away from the masses, begin your trip on big Saganaga Lake and paddle north into Quetico Provincial Park (you can arrange a motorized tow to the edge of the park). For still greater isolation and adventure, try the remote Ontario lakes which lie just outside the Boundary Waters. These Provincial waterways are not subject to BWCA or Quetico park regulations—which means you can camp and build fires where you please. It's doubtful you will see another canoeist.

CHOOSE YOUR ROUTE CAREFULLY

If you're new to the Boundary Waters, you'll want to choose *a wind-protected route that is easy to navigate.* Some great "circle" (no auto shuttle needed) trips originate off the Gunflint Trail, Sawbill Trail and between highway 1 and the Fernberg Road, just southeast of Ely.

MAPS

You may choose from U.S. Geological Survey (U.S.G.S.) and/or Canadian topographic maps, or BWCA/Quetico-specific McKenzie and W.A. Fisher Company Maps. U.S. and Canadian government topo maps are very accurate but they *do not* show the location of portages, campsites and hiking trails in the Boundary Waters and Quetico. For this reason, McKenzie and W.A. Fisher Company maps are preferred.

MCKENZIE COMPANY MAPS

McKenzie maps are drawn on a scale of 2" to the mile (1:31,680), and are printed on nearly indestructible/waterproof POLYART 2 or TYVEK paper. They have crystal clear contour lines and declination diagrams which show the angular difference between true and magnetic north. McKenzie maps are nearly identical to those used by BWCA forest rangers. The 2" to the mile scale makes it is easy to interpret fractional one mile, half mile, and quarter mile distances. McKenzie maps are my personal choice whenever I canoe the Boundary Waters.

W.A. FISHER COMPANY MAPS

W.A. Fisher Company maps are printed on water-proof, polypropylene-based paper. Scales range from 1/3" = 1 mile to 3-1/2" = 1 mile. Most canoeists choose the contoured "F" series maps which are drawn on a scale of 1-1/2" to the mile. Fisher Company offers a nice planning book which contains 15 non-contoured, non-waterproof maps of the BWCA/Quetico.

Write for a free *index* to maps which cover the region you plan to travel. You'll need the *Minnesota* index to order U.S.G.S. topographic maps. Index #1 is required for Ontario provincial maps. McKenzie and W.A. Fisher indexes cover the entire BWCA/Quetico. Procurement information for all maps is in appendix 2.

DON'T TURN YOUR VACATION INTO A MARATHON!

Unless you're a marathon paddler and have a sleek, fast canoe, you'll probably cruise along at around three miles an hour. Subtract one mile per hour of gawking time, photo time and talking time, and you reduce your average to *two miles per hour*. To determine the actual mileage you can cover in a day, you'll have to include time lost on the portages.

Begin by adding up the *total* length, in *rods*, of the portages you will make each day. One rod equals 16.5 feet, or about the length of a typical canoe. *There are 320 rods to the mile*. Most well fit canoeists can portage a canoe 160 rods or half a mile in 10-15 minutes, with one short rest stop. A one mile portage (320 rods) can usually be completed in 20-25 minutes, with two or three rest stops.

Super humans may complete portages in a single grueling carry, but mere mortals like me require *two* trips, which means walking each portage *three* times, once without gear! Long, steep trails require frequent rest stops. Swamps, hills, rain, boulders, overhanging vegetation, and a crowded or precarious landing also slow you down. Some BWCA portages have wooden canoe rests (they will be removed under the new management plan) which allow you to take a breather without setting the canoe down. Where overhead rests don't exist, you'll have to shove the bow of your canoe into a tree or set the craft on the ground. Both procedures waste energy and time. For these reasons, it's probably meaningless to suggest approximate portage times. Nonetheless, these values—which assume you'll retrace your steps three times—work well enough for planning purposes[1]:

[1] It won't take you long to discover that "time under the yoke" is more important than portage length. Note that an easy 320 rod portage may be completed in less time than a tough 240 rod portage!

APPROXIMATE TIME IN MINUTES
TO PORTAGE YOUR GEAR

Map Distance You'll Portage (rods x 3)	Actual Distance	Over a Level, Easy Trail Difficult, Uphill Trail	Over a Moderately Boulders, Rain, Hills, Swamp	Over a Very Difficult Trail:
80 rods or .25 miles	240 rods or .75 miles	15	18	22
160 rods or 0.5 miles	480 rods or 1.5 miles	30	36	44
240 rods or .75 miles	720 rods or 2.25 miles	45	54	66
320 rods or 1.0 miles	960 rods or 3.0 miles	60	72	88

So much for academics. How do you know if a portage and/or route is hard or easy? You don't! But there are some clues. One, is a comparison of the elevation of the lake you're on and the one(s) you'll portage into (figure 2-2). For example, suppose you're located on Warclub Lake (elev. 1693). You plan to paddle up the Chub River and take the short, 45 rod portage into *Glee Lake* (elev. 1729). The difference in elevation is 36 feet over a horizontal distance of 743 feet (45 rods x 16.5 feet per rod). That's 3.6 feet of rise for every 74 feet you walk—pretty significant, even though the portage is only 45 canoe lengths long. Make no mistake, this is a sweaty uphill grade all the way!

You can also check the spacing of the thin, brown *contour lines* on your topographic map. *Contour lines* indicate the elevation above sea level of land features and thus permit you to view the topography in three dimensions instead of two. These rules will help you interpret contour lines:

RULES FOR INTERPRETING CONTOUR LINES

1. Contour lines connect points of equal elevation. Thus, closely spaced lines indicate lots of elevation change, whereas wide-spaced lines show the opposite (figure 2-3). You gain or lose elevation only when you travel from one contour line to another. If you walk along a contour line, you'll be "on the level."

Figure 2-2

Figure 2-3

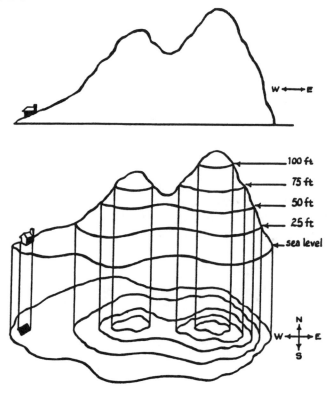

2. The contour interval is the vertical distance in feet or meters between contour lines. Contours on all BWCA area maps are drawn at 20 foot intervals. Thus, you go 20 feet up or down whenever you walk from one contour line to another. Each fifth contour line is darkened and labeled with its actual elevation above sea level.

3. The numerical value of the contour interval (CI) is clearly stated in the margin of all U.S, Canadian, and McKenzie topographic maps, but not on W.A. Fisher Company maps, which are labeled "...not intended for navigational use." An employee of the Fisher Company said that liability concerns required the omission of this important information.

   Caution: No map is 100 percent accurate. River patterns change, water levels rise and fall, trails become overgrown, shorelines erode, campsites come and go. Some U.S. Geological Survey maps—from which most other U.S. maps are made—were last field-checked in the 1950's! No map company can keep up with all the changes imposed by nature and man. Good judgment is essential on any canoe trip!

4. Where contour lines cross or run very close together, you'll find an abrupt drop—a falls, cliff or canyon.

5. A contour line forms a "vee" whenever it crosses a stream or river. The closed end of the "vee" always points upstream. Contours enable you to tell at a glance, the direction of water flow (figure 2-4).

PLANNING THE ROUTE

Now that we have all the facts, let's finish planning our trip. We have decided on a travel zone (Ely, Tofte, Grand Marais...) and a route that sparks our interest. The following "thought list" will help us implement the details of our scenario which, in case you've forgotten, *are seven days on the water, an interesting and diverse route, a few tough portages, five-hour paddling days, relative isolation and one layover day.*

Figure 2-4

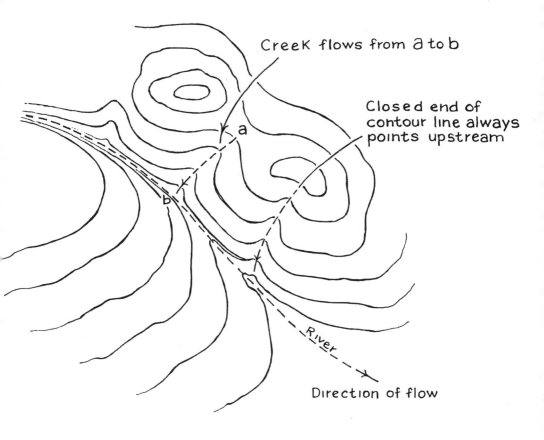

Creek flows from a to b

Closed end of
contour line always
points upstream

Direction of flow

River

SCENARIO THOUGHT LIST
- Have you outlined a circle route that will bring you back to your
  starting point, or arranged for a local outfitter to shuttle your car to
  the take-out? Most BWCA paddlers prefer the freedom of a circle
  route. You can, of course, simply paddle out the same way you came
  in—a less than adventurous experience.
- Most canoe parties begin their trips on a weekend. You'll enjoy a
  less crowded experience if you start on a week day.

- Plan to camp within two hour's paddle of the take-out on your last day. You may be too tired to drive home if you don't!
- Commit mostly to small, easy-to-navigate waters which are protected from high winds. Next year, when you have more confidence, you can try some bigger lakes. There are usually lots of portages (and sometimes more mosquitoes!) along downsized routes, so many canoeists avoid them. The result is a more remote experience for those who are occasionally willing to "sweat and swat." The scenery on sheltered routes is often punctuated with waterfalls, beaver ponds, wildlife sightings and small, runnable rapids—experiences which are foreign to big water.
- Figure on a maximum travel distance of ten miles per day, which includes the "triple carry" length of each portage (you'll walk each portage three times, remember?) you'll make. Add up the length of the portages in rods and multiply by three. Convert this figure to miles (divide rods by 320) and add it to the distance you'll paddle. Say your total is 71 miles. Your "time and distance" schedule might look something like this:

TIME AND DISTANCE SCHEDULE

Day	Time Spent Paddling and Portaging paddling speed= 2 mph. portaging speed = 3 mph	Miles Paddled at 2 mph	Miles Portaged (length of portage x 3)	Total Miles Covered
Day 1 (Tuesday)	4.5 hours	7	3	10 miles
Day 2 (Wednesday)	5 hours	8	3	11 miles
Day 3 (Thursday)	5 hours	6	6	12 miles
Day 4 (Friday)	7 hours	13	1.5	14.5 miles
Day 5 (Saturday)	None-layover day	0	0	0 miles
Day 6 (Sunday)	5 hours	8	3	11 miles
Day 7 (Monday)	4 hours	7	1.5	8.5 miles
Day 8 (Tuesday)	2 hours—out	4	0	4 miles
TOTALS:		53	18	71 miles

Note that you've walked 18 of the 71 miles, or more than 25 percent of the way. This "75/25" ratio is fairly realistic for trips in sheltered waters. You can probably dispense with the foolishness of a "Time and Distance" schedule if you allow *at least* one fourth of your traveling time for portaging! Perhaps now you see why a *lightweight* canoe and outfit are so important!

• Direction of flow: You can go with the current or against it. Your friends want to run some rapids, so you'd best go with the flow. Besides, you can often avoid some portages by selecting a downstream route. Remember, the contour lines tell you the direction of flow; the closed end or tip of the vee always points upstream!

PERMITS

Travel permits are required for canoeing the Boundary Waters. The rules and rationale are explained in chapter 5. For now, you need only know that the maximum party size is *nine* people or *three* canoes. There are no exceptions, even if you paddle a solo canoe or kayak.

The permit system was streamlined in 1994. Now, it's easier than ever to obtain a travel permit. Direct permit requests to:

BWCA Reservation Service
P.O. Box 450
Cumberland, Maryland 21501
Phone 1-800-745-3399

All permits cost $7.00 and may be charged to VISA, Mastercard or Discover. Permits are available on the following basis:

RESERVED OVERNIGHT PERMITS

You may reserve these permits weeks or months before your trip. You will receive computerized verification of your travel dates, entry point and route. Unless you specify otherwise, your permit will be waiting for you at the Forest Service office closest to your entry point. You must pick up your permit in person (bring the letter of confirmation) within 24 hours of your trip.

RESERVED DAY-USE MOTOR PERMITS

This permit allows you to use a motor on your canoe for *one* day during the week of your canoe trip. Weeks run Saturday to Friday. Be sure you have the confirmation letter with you when you pick up your permit.

WALK-IN OVERNIGHT AND DAY-USE MOTOR PERMITS

Stop at any Forest Service district office or any cooperating outfitter within 24 hours of your trip. If a permit is available, one will be issued to you.

YOU MUST LICENSE YOUR CANOE IN MINNESOTA

Your canoe must be licensed with the Minnesota Department of Natural Resources, unless it has already been licensed in another state, in which case, there must be an official decal affixed to the hull. Canoe licenses are available by mail from the Minnesota Department of Natural Resources, License Bureau, 500 Lafayette Square, St. Paul, MN 55146, and from some local outfitters. Call the DNR's toll free number (1-800-285-2000) for a list of participating outfitters. The cost is $12.00 for three years.

If you are renting a canoe in Minnesota, it has already been licensed.

ENTRY INTO CANADA'S QUETICO PROVINCIAL PARK

Unlike the Boundary Waters, there are no designated campsites, fire-places or maintained toilets in the interior of Quetico Provincial Park. The maximum group size is nine people and there is no restriction on the number of canoes per party. The interior of Quetico park is much wilder than the most remote parts of the BWCA.

Park reservations are accepted by mail beginning January 18, and by phone starting February 1st. Inquiries about entry points, canoeing and camping regulations, permits, fees, licenses and customs procedures should be addressed to:

Reservations
Quetico Provincial Park
Ministry of Natural Resources
Atikokan, Ontario
Canada POT 1CO
Phone: (807) 597-2735

Park fees vary according to age (youth, adult or senior citizen), season and facilities used. There's a daily parking charge for vehicles. You'll need to buy an Ontario angling license if you plan to fish. And you *must* check through Canadian customs before you enter the park. Customs stations are located on Saganaga Lake (Cache Bay), Basswood Lake (Prairie Portage), and Sand Point Lake. Everything is clearly explained in the free brochure, *Welcome to Quetico Provincial Park*, which is available from the MNR office at the address above.

Your planning is now complete. All that remains is to assemble your food and gear and learn how to use your newly acquired maps to find your way around the sprawling lakes you'll soon encounter.

CHAPTER THREE

A Maze of Finger Lakes, Portage Trails and Confusing Bays!

Newcomers to the Boundary Waters secretly admit a deep fear of being unable to find designated campsites and portages. Anxiety grows to ulcer proportions when bad weather carves hours out of a tight time schedule. To eliminate confusion, some novices simply glue their route to a shoreline or camp within sight of their starting point or a portage. Others pack away their map and compass and paddle off confidently in the general direction of their goal without giving the matter a second thought.

During the peak of the canoeing season, you can probably get around fine with these attitudes if you have a friendly smile and a willingness to ask directions of other paddlers you meet. But you won't grow with the sport or develop much confidence in your route-finding ability. More importantly, you may lock yourself out of traveling the most remote portions of the Boundary Waters, where good map and compass reading is essential.

Ask an experienced canoeist for directions and you will almost always be politely and cheerfully accommodated. You will, however, be viewed as an incompetent bozo who doesn't know the ropes and isn't willing to take the time to learn!

Admittedly, the BWCA is not an easy place to find your way around. The maze of islands, bays and channels, combined with portage trails which are sometimes incorrectly plotted on maps, often confuses experts who have superior map and compass skills. Indeed, my own experience on the sprawling waterways of northern Canada suggests that if you can correctly navigate complex Boundary Waters lakes like Seagull and Saganaga, you can probably find your way around any liquid habitat in the world. The BWCA may be small potatoes compared to the giant lakes of northern Canada, but the rules for navigating them are the same. A good map, a reliable *Orienteering* compass and an understanding of basic route-finding principles will eliminate confusion.

ESSENTIAL EQUIPMENT

Maps

Get the best maps available. I prefer the large scale McKenzie maps suggested in chapter 2. Losing a map can be serious, so always carry one or two spares. Best place to store your map is in a sturdy nylon map case, under a "shock-corded" canoe thwart, as suggested in chapter 6. Excellent map cases are available from Cooke Custom Sewing, Grade VI and Granite Gear. Addresses are in appendix 2.

ORIENTEERING COMPASS

If you've never used an *Orienteering* compass, you have a pleasant surprise coming. You don't have to write down numbers, memorize dial readings or draw north-south reference lines on your map. The features you need for computing map bearings, and following them on the ground are built right into the instrument!

Silva, Suunto and Brunton all make excellent Orienteering compasses. Prices range from about ten dollars to more than forty for professional models which feature declination adjustments, night sights and interchangeable map scales. But, you don't need any of these sophisticated features for navigating the Boundary Waters! The least expensive Orienteering compasses are adequate for serious route-finding.

Inexpensive Orienteering compasses are usually lighter and more compact than large frame professional models—an advantage when you have to carry them all day in your pants pocket. My favorite Boundary Waters compass is the tiny (and inexpensive) *Silva Huntsman*, which is scarcely larger than a book of paper matches.

Carry a spare compass, "just in case." A small wrist compass that straps or Velcroes™ to a canoe thwart provides instant bearings while you paddle. A thwart-mounted "running" compass simplifies direction finding and may even promote your safe passage. For example, say you're following a compass heading across a windy lake. You paddle around an island and momentarily lose track of your direction. If you put down your paddle and reach for your Orienteering compass to check the course, you may broadside the waves and swamp. Fortunately, your thwart-mounted "running" compass shows the way.

Figure 3-1

NO NEED TO WORRY ABOUT MAGNETIC DECLINATION!

A compass needle points to *magnetic* north, not *true* north. The angular difference between the "two norths" is called "declination." In some areas of the United States—notably the far east and west, declination can be as much as 21 degrees! Fortunately, declination in the Boundary Waters Canoe Area and adjacent Quetico Provincial Park is so small (it ranges from about three degrees at the eastern edge of the BWCA to a bit more than four degrees at the western boundary) that you can ignore it.

For example: One degree of compass error equals 92 feet per mile of ground error. Say you shoot a compass bearing from your location to a point one-half mile away. This is a fairly long compass shot, given the small size of most Boundary Waters lakes. Figure in an area maximum declination of four degrees east, and you would be off course a maximum of 184 feet (92 feet per mile x 4° x 0.5 miles) or about half the length of a football field—hardly enough to cause concern.

So rest easy, *there is no need to correct compass readings for declination in the BWCA!*

USING MAP AND COMPASS TOGETHER

In order to locate portages and campsites, you must know, within reason, where you are at all times. This means you must proceed along an established direction, or "bearing" as it is called.

Assume you are camped at point A on Whiskey Jack Lake (figure 3-1). Your destination is portage X in the southwest corner of Trout Bay. Getting to X should be easy: Just head southwest through the channel at B, then curve around Moose Island until you come to the lake expanse. Now turn south, cross to the opposite shore and follow your nose to the portage. Easy as pie!

Figure 3-2

Don't you believe it! Look at the map scale. It's about three eighths of a mile to the channel at B, and nearly a full mile from Moose Island to the mainland at G. Even on a clear day, it's hard to discern the nature of islands, channels and bays which are hundreds of yards away. Add morning fog, wind and waves, plus the sight and sounds of unfamiliar surroundings and you could easily become confused. Better to resort to precise compass bearings and follow a systematic plan. The important thing is *to know your location at all times*—easy enough if you compute compass bearings to intermediate check points (B, C, D, E, etc.) along the way and verify your position when you arrive at each point. Here's the procedure:

First, arbitrarily pick a check point on the map. It should be some place that's reasonably close (preferably within one-half mile of your location) and easily identifiable—a small island, the tip of a peninsula, a prominent bay, etc. You probably won't be able to see your check point from your distant location.

Let's say that the island at B (the dot marks the point) is your first check point. Don't touch your compass until you first estimate (within 90°) the bearing from A to B. You'll be heading roughly west, so your computed compass bearing should be around 270°.

Now, use your Orienteering compass to determine the actual compass bearing from A to B. Figure 3-2 shows the procedure:

1. Place either the left or right edge of the compass base plate over point A. Place the forward edge of the same side of the base plate on point B. Your compass is now pointing in the direction you want to go—from A to B, not from B to A!

2. While holding the base plate tightly in position, *turn the compass housing* until north on the dial points to north (the top) on the map. *Caution:* Don't use the magnetic needle! Your direction of travel—256°—is now locked on the dial and can be read at the index inscribed on the compass base.

STOP IMMEDIATELY. DO NOT CONTINUE UNTIL YOU HAVE COMPARED YOUR COMPUTED 256° COMPASS BEARING TO YOUR EARLIER ESTIMATE OF 270°! The most common mistakes are *quadrant* (90° to 180°) and full 180° errors. You'll avoid these embarrassing mistakes if you compare your calculated bearing to your estimate *before* you start paddling! The two figures should closely agree.

Your calculated bearing of *256°* is within 45° of your 270° estimate, so it's unlikely you made a serious mistake.

It's easier to make a large computational error than you think! For example, if you inadvertently place your compass wrong on the map or turn the north arrow on the housing *down* (South) instead of up (North), your computed bearing may be off as much as 180 degrees!

Now...while holding the compass in front of you with the direction-of-travel arrow inscribed on the base plate pointing *away* from your body, rotate your body *with the compass* until the magnetic needle points to north on the dial. Look straight ahead. You are now facing 256 degrees—towards B.

4. All that's necessary now is to locate a notch or incongruity on the horizon that you can identify as being on this course of travel. Put your compass away and start paddling! *Caution:* Wind may blow your canoe off course, so *don't* follow a bearing set on your thwart mounted compass. Instead, select a point on the horizon that is in line with the bearing you computed with your Orienteering compass.

Test time! Use your Orienteering compass and figure 3-1 to test your knowledge of "point to point" navigation. Remember to *estimate* the bearing to each point before you compute it! Consider your answers correct if they are within three degrees of those given in figure 3-3 at the end of this chapter.

If you can successfully navigate Whiskey Jack Lake, you'll be "on course" on your next canoe trip. That's a promise!

AIMING OFF

Maps are made from aerial photos, and the plane-mounted camera can only record what it sees. Man-made features like portages are often obscured by trees, so the cartographer has to guess at precise locations. As water levels fluctuate, shorelines change shape. The result is that what you see on the map may not accurately represent what is on the ground. To locate a mis-plotted feature, you'll need to "aim-off."

For example: You are located at point I on Whiskey Jack Lake (figure 3-1), and you want to go to portage X. If this portage is incorrectly plotted on the map, or you make a small compass error, you could miss your objective. Err much to the south and you could even mistake portage Y for X!

The solution is to "aim off"—that is, make a purposeful error to the right or left of X. In the example, an arbitrary point (Z) was selected. Determine the bearing from I to Z and start paddling! You will intersect the shoreline somewhere *north* of X. Follow the shore south to the first portage you come to. That's X. What could be simpler?

"Aim off" whenever you use your compass and you won't spend hours searching for portages!

TIPS FOR NAVIGATING SMALL STREAMS AND MOOSE TRAILS

Sometimes you can bypass portages by following a connecting stream or moose trail to the next lake. Here are some hints for navigating these meandering waterways:

1. Where a stream forks, take the route with the strongest flow, even if it looks more restrictive than a broader channel. If there's no discernible current, note which way the grass bends in the channel and follow.
2. Check your compass frequently; Don't rely on your map!
3. If you come to a dead end and see a trail, scout it before you carry your canoe across. Your "portage" may turn out to be an animal path which leads to a connecting tributary or dead-end pond.

Figure 3-3

ANSWERS

FROM	YOUR GUESTIMATE	ACTUAL COMPASS BEARING
A to B	SW (180°-270°)	256°
B to C	SW (180°-270°)	237°
C to D	SW (180°-270°)	216°
D to E	S (about 180°)	196°
E to F	SE (90° -180°)	162°
F to G	SW (180°-270°)	211°
G to H	SW (180°-270°)	217°
H to I	SW (180°-270°)	217°
I to Z, just north of portage X[1]	SW (180°-270°)	234°

[1]Note that this bearing was computed to an arbitrary point (Z) just north of portage X. This procedure, called "aiming off" prevents undershooting or overshooting your objective. You'll find the rationale for this method on page 25.

CHAPTER FOUR

Favorite Routes - Where Solitude Still Remains

I live on the Minnesota border where snow stays on the ground from November to May. When melt water finally comes to Viking land, there's cause for serious applause. Canoes and camping gear which have laid dormant all winter are suddenly the focus of attention, as everyone prepares for the elusive summer. May 15, start of the fishing opener, officially marks the end of the ice age in Minnesota, and the first big influx of visitors to the BWCA. Fortunately, most serious anglers limit their casts to large, accessible lakes like Rainy, Vermillion, Basswood, Seagull and Saganaga, where motors are permitted and portages are non-existent. That leaves lots of space for winter-crazed paddlers like me who want to get away from the maddening crowd.

Long, tough portages once separated serious backwoods travelers from wilderness weenies. Today, lightweight gear has evened the score—a one-mile portage is easy if you have a 50 pound canoe and Spartan kit. Just about everyone who canoes the Boundary Waters these days has discovered the lightweight advantage. Those who haven't are quickly set straight by area outfitters who offer the latest in ultra-light gear. "Getting away from it all" now means probing deeper into the wilderness than ever before, or cleverly skirting the beaten path (more on this later).

You *can* find solitude in the Boundary Waters if you portage into a dead-end lake, pond-hop between beaver streams and/or select a route that includes hard-to-portage rapids. Whitewater terrifies unskilled paddlers, especially those who have sleek, fragile cruising canoes which turn reluctantly. Deviate from the programmed portage path (even momentarily!) and you'll discover that there's a wild and wooly side to the BWCA.

Here are a few of my favorite haunts and some adventurous ways to get away from the crowd:

HAM LAKE TO LONG ISLAND LAKE AND POINTS EAST

(Three to seven days)
Maps needed: McKenzie #7 and #4, or Fisher #114 or F13 and F6

Here's a diverse route for those who prefer small, easily navigable (you can't get lost!), wind-protected lakes which have nice campsites, good fishing and lots of wildlife.

Figure 4-1

Enter at Ham Lake (map illustration 4-1) off the Gunflint Trail near Grand Marais. It's an easy day's paddle to Long Island Lake, via Cross Bay, Rib, George and Karl Lakes. There's a long sand beach (rare, in this region of uninterrupted granite!) at the end of the 35 rod portage from Karl Lake to Long Island Lake.

If you want a more remote experience, exit Long Island Lake to the east and paddle into Ross, Banadad and Rush Lake. Or, drop down into Muskeg, Omega, Hensen and Pillsberry. Loop back to Long Island Lake through Winchell and Davis, or cut south to big Brule Lake, and return by way of Cam, Town and Cherokee Lakes. Surrounded by high granite cliffs, tiny Cam Lake looks like a crater hole from the seat of a canoe. It is one of the most beautiful and unusual spots in the area. A number of tight, annoying portages keep most people away.

The skinny streams which feed Long Island Lake are prime habitat for beaver, moose, otter and muskrat. The region feels comfortably intimate—a perfect place for adventurous beginners who are just spreading their wings.

FROST RIVER (map illustration 4-2)

(Five to seven days)
Maps : McKenzie #7 and #8, or Fisher #113 and #114 or F-12, F-13, F-19

The Frost River has a smattering of everything—large and small lakes, beautiful falls, winding beaver streams and high beaver dams, tough, poorly maintained portages, canoeable rapids and adventurous options. It is by far my favorite route in the Boundary Waters.

The Frost River is rugged and isolated. You'll enjoy the trip more if you have lightweight gear, a compact kit and an unhurried attitude. You'll paddle downhill all the way and enjoy a number of easy rapids. Campsites are limited on the Frost River portion of the route, so you'd best plan your stays accordingly. The trip *must* be done in early June or late September when water levels are reasonably high.

Expect to see lots of wildlife. When my wife, Susie and I paddled the Frost in our solo canoes in June 1993, we saw five otters, one beaver, several muskrats, a white-tailed deer (!) and two huge bull moose. We were too rushed to fish, though on past trips (I've paddled the Frost at least a dozen times), we've nabbed some nice smallmouth bass and northern pike.

Park your car at the Round Lake public landing (map illustration 4-1), and begin your trip at Ham Lake, a five-minute walk to the east. Paddle south to Long Island Lake then take the 140 rod portage into Frost Lake. This portage is long and mean so I usually camp at Long Island or Gordon Lake and save the sweaty carry for the next morning. There are only two campsites between Frost Lake and the mouth of the river at Afton Lake. Bologna Lake, which is accessed by a short, ten rod portage has one campsite, and it's a knockout!

The Frost River valley is well protected from wind and the sounds of other paddlers. There are several small waterfalls, rapids and beaver dams to portage. You'll thread your way through miles of head-high plants which resemble wild rice beds, twisting and turning with the restricted flow. Fortunately, beavers and moose maintain a tight but navigable channel.

Figure 4-2

In good weather, it's a 12-14 hour run from Frost Lake to Little Saganaga Lake, and you'll spoil the fun if you do it all in a single day. The winding Frost River is so remote and inspiring that two days seem hardly enough for those who will contemplate and explore the waterway. Only one portage intersects the river—a grueling 300 rodder out of Hub Lake. Fellow voyageurs are either behind you or ahead and gone.

At Whipped Lake, you may choose to head north to Mora, Gillis, Chub River and Brant, ending your trip at Round Lake. Or, proceed north to Gabimichigami, Ogishkemuncie, Jasper, Alpine and Seagull.

The first option is much more remote and adventurous, especially, if you bypass the 100 rod portage to Mora and take the obscure Time Lake cut-off. The rapids and swifts between Whipped and Mora Lakes can all be run, lined or portaged. Be sure you have ropes attached to the bow and stern of your canoe!

Little Saganaga Lake is one of the most beautiful in the Boundary Waters. It is well worth seeing, even though it is very heavily traveled. You're on big water now, as you loop north towards famed Seagull Lake. The country is gorgeous, portages are easy and there are plenty of other canoeists around. "Remote" defines country you've left behind! Any of the area's outfitters will shuttle your car from Ham Lake to Seagull for a small charge.

GRANITE RIVER THROUGH GUIDE'S PORTAGE
(map illustration 4-3)

Three to five days: Access via Gunflint Trail, north of Grand Marais)

The Granite River is one of the most beautiful and satisfying routes in the Boundary Waters. Portages are short and well maintained, the high granite bluffs discourage wind and the high relief topography is truly spectacular. It's a downstream run all the way to Saganaga Lake which, for all practical purposes is the only big water on the route. The route is easy to navigate.

The downside is that *lots* of very inexperienced people canoe the Granite River. In fact, just about every tripping camp in the region sends its teen groups down the Granite. Use—and abuse—is heavy. Most of the "good wood" on campsites has been picked over, and more often than not, campsites are at or nearly at full capacity. Nonetheless, the Granite River is so rewarding that you'll want to paddle it more than once.

Begin your trip at the public landing on Gunflint Lake. Arrange with Gunflint Lodge to shuttle your car to Trails End Landing on Saganaga Lake. Paddle north to Pine Portage but *don't* carry into Clove Lake. Instead, descend through a small swift and follow the *main body of the river* into a quiet pool which dead-ends about 100 yards above Clove Lake. An unkempt portage begins on river left (the American side) at the head of a rapid. The rapid ends at a substantial falls, below which is one of the most beautiful spots—and best swimming holes—I've seen. Near the left shore, a natural bathtub is carved into the hard, smooth granite. You can't camp at the falls, but you can picnic, swim and nap.

Follow the portage to the quiet pool below the falls. Then, paddle across the pool to the Canadian side and hoist your outfit about ten feet up the rock embankment to the overgrown trail above. A five-minute walk down this "Guide's Portage" brings you to Clove Lake. Most people take the 100 rod portage directly to Clove Lake and miss the falls which, I think, is the prettiest spot on the Granite River.

"Guide's Portage" was named for the commercial guides who, decades ago, brought clients here to fish below the falls. The area is fragile, so please pass through quietly and clean and carry out any mess you find. In return, you'll experience one of the premier attractions of the Boundary Waters Canoe Area.

At the end of Clove Lake is an innocuous looking rapid. A fast right turn is needed to get around the midstream boulder which sits in the heart of the flowing water. *Study* this rapid before you attempt it. Better yet, take the good portage on river left!

As you proceed down river, you'll come to several small rapids which are bypassed by easy portages. Many of the rapids can be run if you have whitewater experience. **Caution: *Do not*** run any rapid until you have walked its length, checked every turn and rock and discussed "possible outcomes" with your partner!

Follow the Granite River to Saganaga Lake, then swing west and south and paddle to your take-out point at Trails End landing.

Earlier in this chapter, I suggested that the Boundary Waters has a wild and wooly side that comes to light whenever you leave the beaten path. Many rapids, swifts and beaver streams which are rotely portaged by unadventurous canoeists can, after careful inspection, be safely canoed, lined or waded—an example is the "Time Lake cutoff" suggested earlier.

Follow a beaver stream to a dead-end lake, set a compass course and hike overland to a landlocked pond, climb some high hills and, as John Muir proclaimed, "Get their good tidings." Slow your pace, shorten your trip plans, investigate your options, probe shorelines, quiet bays and the thin lines on your map, and you'll discover challenge and solitude wherever you paddle.

Figure 4-3

CHAPTER FIVE

Federal Regulations & Rationale

*"Every part of the earth is sacred to my people.
Every shining pine needle, every sandy shore,
every mist in the dark woods, every clearing and humming insect
is holy in the memory and experience of my people."*

Chief Sealth (Seattle), from a speech delivered
to representatives of the United States government in 1855.

Autumn mist on an isolated lake deep in the Boundary Waters Canoe Area—one last paddle trip before the icy throes of winter—a final opportunity to camp and fish and to enjoy the good times that go with warm friendships and fire-brewed coffee served steaming hot on a chilly morning.

'Round the bend is the campsite which you discovered more than a decade ago. Hauntingly beautiful, it is your "special" place. You pull your canoe up on shore and follow the well-worn trail to the clearing above. The view from on top is spectacular, just as you remembered it.

Then you see them—rusty cans, aluminum foil and candy wrappers. Torn plastic sheeting, secured to knotted nylon cord, flutters from a white birch tree, whose bark has been stripped to start campfires. At the center of the stage is the steel fire grate which is choked with green cedar branches and pine needles. Nearby, deep eroded ruts suggest that those who last camped here "ditched" their tents to drain storm water.

Suddenly, this place is no longer special. It is a trash heap, an insult to man and God. A gnawing pain grows upward from the pit of your stomach and surfaces as rage. The spell is broken!

Fortunately, trashed campsites like these are uncommon in the Boundary Waters. Environmental regulations which are strictly enforced, plus a growing educational effort by federal authorities have eliminated most abuse. Many canoeists share an almost religious view of the Boundary Waters. They willingly clean up after themselves and others, taking personal pride as their only reward. The "bottle and can" ban has all but eliminated this once prominent eye-sore, but many of the old problems—candy wrappers, aluminum foil, stripped birch bark, vegetation-choked fire-grates and cut green trees—remain.

The "rules of travel" accompany every permit, and visitors are encouraged (newcomers are *required!*) to see and reflect on a variety of educational videos, pamphlets and photos which define low impact camping techniques. Nonetheless, the exposure is too fast and badly timed. Wilderness education should take place in a more relaxed setting, days or weeks in advance of the outdoor experience. This is especially true where teenagers are concerned. Kids often forget what they learned within a matter of days (hours!) unless they actively review the material.

The key to mastery is practice, practice and more practice, *before* paddles touch water. To this end, I offer a unique "Wilderness Meal" cook-out (see appendix 4) which I developed for use in my eighth grade environmental science classes. Kids (and adults!) love this non-intimidating "hands on" activity, which gets at the heart of wilderness ethics. My publisher graciously permits you to copy the materials for educational purposes, in any numbers you wish.

In order to provide a quality outdoor experience for everyone, *everyone* must understand the rationale behind each rule. They must also be armed with "alternatives" to choosing environmentally unsound ways. For example: How do you keep storm water out of your tent if you can't dig a trench around it? Or, make a cheery fire without using birch bark and cedar foliage? If campers know how to tie *quick-release* (slippery) knots that come out with a single pull, they probably won't leave knotted cord hanging from trees! Suppose that, due to circumstances beyond your control, you must camp overnight at an unapproved site. It happens! Once a tornado-like gale with winds to 65 miles per hour pinned my teenage crew on a lonely shoreline for eighteen hours. Given this scenario, how do you cook, sleep, answer the call of nature and get out of the weather without mucking up the environment? Every Boundary Waters canoeist should know the answers to these questions and be skilled in applying *environmentally correct* solutions!

Regrettably, governmental agencies continue to legislate much more than they educate, but there are encouraging signs on the wind. The final Environmental Impact Statement (EIS) and BWCA Wilderness Management Plan and Implementation Schedule (WMPIS) released to the public on August 19, 1993—and, at this writing, still awaiting approval—promises that "there will be increased emphasis on visitor education." The EIS/WMPIS also includes a number of significant changes that, if approved, should improve the wilderness experience for everyone. What follows is a brief overview of the most important concerns, and the rationale behind them.

PARTY SIZE AND NUMBER OF CANOES

Prior to 1995, a maximum of 382 groups of up to ten people each, were allowed to enter the Boundary Water's 86 entry points each day. Starting in 1995, this figure will be reduced to 280.

U.S. Forest Service "Wilderness Specialist" Barb Soderberg urges canoeists not to overreact to the new policy. She points out that, on average, 203 groups enter the Boundary Waters daily, so the new regulation should only come into play at high use entry points and during holiday weekends and mid-summer peak use periods. Soderberg thinks the result will be "a more remote, less frustrating experience for everyone." *Quotas will continue to remain in effect only during the permit season, which runs from May 1 to September 30.*

Further restrictions take effect in January, 1995 and apply throughout the year. These include special (different) permits for the October through April off season and a reduction in party size and number of watercraft per party. *Maximum group size, which is currently ten, will drop to nine*, which is identical to that in Quetico Provincial Park. *And no more than three canoes may travel together or be beached on shore.* Solo canoes? "Three means three!" says Soderberg. "If you have more than three boats in your group, you're in violation of the law!"

Note that the maximum party size regulation applies *everywhere* in the BWCA— on campsites, portages, and while traveling on the water. The law is rigidly enforced!

NO CANS OR BOTTLES ARE ALLOWED IN THE BWCA!

Foods and medicines are the only exception to this rule. Nonburnable, disposable food and beverage containers are not allowed. Rigging a #10 tin can with a coat-hanger bail and using it as a cooking pot, is not legal!

CAMP ONLY AT U.S. FOREST SERVICE DESIGNATED SITES

Shown as "red dots" on McKenzie and Fisher Company maps, designated campsites have box latrines, fire grates and cleared tent spots. Stay away from campsites which are closed (a sign is erected)! The reason for closure my be overuse and/or dangerous water pollution—human waste from the box latrine may have seeped into the lake and contaminated the water. *Never swim or take drinking water from areas near closed campsites!* You'll find more particulars about water pollution and purification in chapter 12.

WHEN NATURE CALLS AND THERE IS NO FOREST SERVICE BOX LATRINE

When nature calls and there is no box latrine, do this: Go at least 150 feet from water, well away from campsites and portage trails. Dig a shallow (two to six inches) hole with the heel of your boot. When you have finished, burn the toilet paper and *thoroughly douse* the flames with water from your poly bottle. *Caution:* Well-meaning campers have started forest fires by burning toilet paper. *Do not* burn toilet paper if you don't have a water bottle! Cover human waste and *dead out* fire remains with two to six inches of soil. That's all there is to it!

Rationale for this procedure: Human waste and *burned* toilet paper degrade quickly if microbes are present. The top six inches of soil contain the greatest number of decay organisms. Forest Service box latrines are environmentally unsound because they concentrate fecal matter in deep, rocky soil where there is little bacterial action. Nonetheless, box latrines are the preferred method of waste disposal because few campers willingly embrace the "heel-scrape/burn toilet paper" procedure suggested above.

CAMPFIRES ARE ALLOWED ONLY WITHIN THE STEEL FIRE GRATES AT DEVELOPED CAMPSITES

This thoroughly sensible rule is seldom violated in the BWCA. However, a secure place to contain fire is one thing; the *ability* to make it—especially in rain, is another. When repeated attempts to make fire fail, frustrated campers often strip birch bark and cedar boughs from living trees. Often, they chop or saw fully grown, live trees. My own experience suggests that *saws* have replaced axes as the favored tool of destruction. On a recent BWCA solo canoe trip, I counted fourteen sawn green trees around my camp on Bat Lake (Gunflint Trail area)!

In severe weather, a professional outdoors person, armed with matches and a Swiss Army knife, may need thirty minutes or more to establish a reliable campfire. Given the same situation and tools, a novice camper may be lucky to get smoke. In chapter 10 you'll discover how a hand axe—the carrying of which is heavily discouraged by Boundary Waters authorities—can simplify fire making and thereby *eliminate* environmental damage to living foliage. Alternatives are available for those who are willing to listen!

AN UNATTENDED FIRE IS SERIOUS CAUSE FOR CONCERN

Just about every experienced canoeist at one time or other has passed a campsite with an actively burning campfire and no one to guard it. Since you can't control a campfire you can't see, any activity which takes everyone away from the fire site is a breach of safety and a violation of law. Leaving a fire unattended, even for short periods of time, is something that Forest Service personnel take very seriously!

BE SURE YOUR FIRE IS DEAD OUT BEFORE YOU LEAVE CAMP!

Douse your campfire with plenty of water and stir the ashes to a thick slush that exudes *no smoke or steam*. Then, check the slurry *with your hand*. A popular rule is that "if the ashes are hot enough to burn your hand, they are hot enough to burn a forest!"

SANITATION AND WASTE DISPOSAL

Before you retire, your food supply should be double-sealed in plastic and secured in your buckled Duluth pack. The food pack should be taken *out of the immediate camp area* and hidden in the woods, among rocks along the shore, or treed, per the instructions in chapter 11.

The best way to dispose of uneaten food is to burn it. Build a good, hot fire so that the remains of foodstuffs won't extinguish the blaze. Burn garbage *completely*, and be sure to pick aluminum foil out of the flames before it melts all over everything. Partially melted foil has become the scourge of the Boundary Waters!

Soupy leftovers and fish entrails can be a problem. If you throw them in the lake, germ counts rise and dissolved oxygen levels fall. For this reason, "burial by water" is illegal in Minnesota and in most other places. Best method is to bury biodegradable wastes under four to six inches of soil, well away from camp, 150 feet from water. A heavy rock or log placed atop the buried remains will help discourage animals. On very isolated lakes, fish viscera may be placed on a large boulder well away from designated campsites and human habitation. Sea gulls will appreciate the meal.

Dishes should be washed on land, well away from the water's edge. Ditto bathing and shampooing hair. Take dirty bathwater *out of the campsite area, 150 feet from the lake*, and pour it into the ground. Greasy dishwater is best poured into a shallow hole and covered with soil. Detergents should be biodegradable and sparingly used.

ADMINISTRATIVE CONCERNS

The proposed BWCA Wilderness Management Plan contains a number of decisions that are primarily administrative and discretionary. The following ones are most likely to be implemented.

- There will be increased emphasis on visitor education.
- Daily overnight quotas will not be overbooked as has been the case in the past.
- Permits canceled more than 24 hours prior to the trip starting date will become available for reissue.
- Permit reservations will be accepted between January 15 and September 30.
- Personal identification is required to pick up a permit.
- Permits for day and overnight use (regardless of mode of travel) will be required year long.
- Associated groups may not travel together but may use the same route.
- All members of a party must camp on the same site.
- Sailboats and sailboards are prohibited.

- Special Use Permits (Outfitter-Guide License) will be required for everyone who guides private individuals, school, church and camp groups. Of course, there's a "processing fee." It's geared to the number of clients and the number of days out. Back in the mid-1970's, our school district was required to obtain outfitter-guide licenses for staff personnel who led trips into the Boundary Waters. There was a lot of red tape and expense involved, and no check on leadership competency. Anyone who filled out the papers and paid the money got a license. The U.S. Forest Service in Duluth can provide the essential forms.
- All competitive events (like canoe and dog sled races) are prohibited.
- Dogs will be required to be under voice or leash control.
- Wooden canoe rests will be removed.

The Forest Service plans to implement these ideas after the 1994 use season.

At the start of this chapter, I mentioned "alternatives" to environmentally unsound ways. You'll find a wealth of these procedures in the chapters that follow.

Figure 6-1

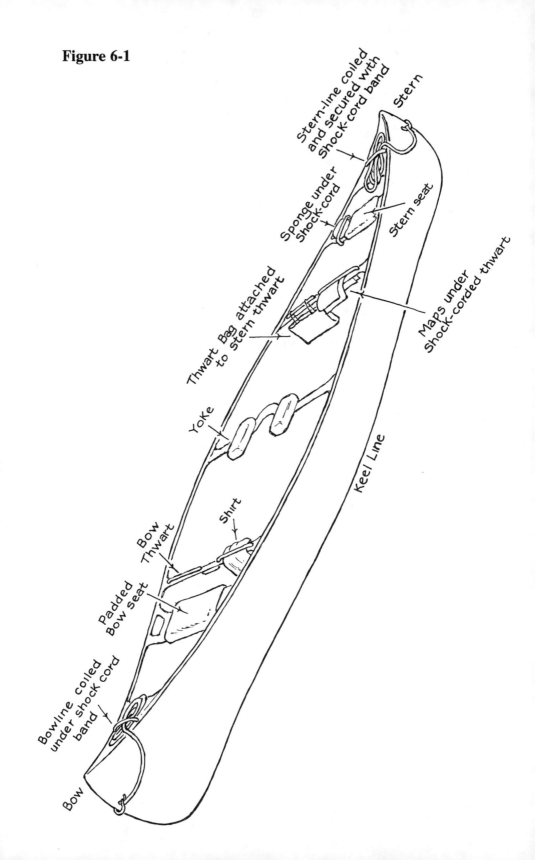

Stern-line coiled and secured with Shock-cord band

Stern

Sponge under Shock-cord

Stern seat

Maps under Shock-corded thwart

Thwart Bag attached to stern thwart

Yoke

Keel Line

Bow Thwart

Shirt

Padded Bow seat

Bowline coiled under shock cord band

Bow

CHAPTER SIX

Selecting & Outfitting
Your Canoe

A BOUNDARY WATERS CANOE CAN NEVER BE
"TOO LIGHT"!

Where the lakes end, the portages begin. They go up and down hills, over boulder fields and through swamps. Often, you must hop from rock to rock or slosh hundreds of yards through knee-high muck, balancing your canoe and swatting mosquitoes as you go. You may repeat this scenario half a dozen times on a typical day in the Boundary Waters. If you want to keep a merry disposition, you'll paddle a *very light canoe!*

How light is *very light*? Sixty-five pounds is reasonable, 55 or less is a blessing. Tripping canoes are available which weigh under 50 pounds. Look into them if you want to treat your body kindly.

Surprisingly, a very small reduction in canoe weight makes a big difference on the portage trail. Alternately carry a 65 pound and 60 pound canoe over the same portage and you'll marvel at the contrast. Try the same experiment with a loaded packsack and you'll be less impressed. Why? Because all the weight of the pack is born by your torso, while that of the canoe is spread along the length of the hull, which affects its "swing weight" or momentum. The effect is most punishing on a tight, twisting portage where you must hop from rock to rock.

A FAST CANOE IS A WELCOME LUXURY

A fast canoe is a luxury, given the small lakes and frequent portages which dominate the Boundary Waters. For example, a good crew can cover a mile in a long, lean canoe in twelve to fourteen minutes. Another minute or two may be needed to propel a shorter, pushier craft—a small concern when everyone is on vacation and out for a good time.

On the other hand, it's nice to have a canoe that paddles easily, especially when you're pushing into a strong head-wind. Fortunately, lightweight canoes are usually fast canoes. Why? Because lightweight construction is expensive, so few manufacturers will waste it on bad design.

The variables which affect "ease-of-paddling" and "speed" are too complex to detail here (see my books, *Canoeing & Camping* and *Canoeing Wild Rivers* for specifics). However, these rules always apply:

1. Long, skinny canoes are faster and easier to paddle than short, fat canoes. They also stay on course better in wind.
2. A keel is not necessary to keep a canoe on course. Indeed, a keel is usually the sign of an inferior canoe! Aluminum canoes which are formed in two halves and require a longitudinal brace along the bottom, are the exception. The Indians and voyageurs did not have keels on their canoes, so why should we? Straight tracking (the ability to stay on course in wind) is largely a function of long waterline length, fine ends, and a slender, rounded or vee-shaped hull form.
3. Given: Two identical canoes, one light, one heavy. The lighter canoe will accelerate faster and require less effort to maintain its speed. Only when driving forward into a headwind is the momentum of a heavier canoe an advantage.

CANOE BUILDING MATERIALS

Royalex and polyethylene are the preferred materials for canoes that will be used on rocky rivers. But we're paddling lake country, remember? A Boundary Waters cruiser should be light and quick— features which largely favor Kevlar™, fiberglass, and wood-strip construction. However, recent advances in fabrication techniques now make Royalex™ a viable competitor. Check out the sleek new Royalex™ cruising canoes from Dagger, Old Town, Mad River and others, and you'll see how far this material has come.

TIPS

1. If you want to round up a great Boundary Waters canoe but don't want to research hull designs, look hard at keel-less, lightweight canoes which are 17-1/2 to 18-1/2 feet long. These craft are usually designed for serious paddlers.

2. Wood gunnels, seats and thwarts are usually much lighter than aluminum and plastic trim. The difference may amount to as much as ten pounds on the typical 17 foot canoe! And contrary to popular belief, maintenance of wood-trimmed boats is easy. Store your craft out of direct sun and rain, occasionally rub in some Djeks Olay™, linseed or Watco oil, and the craft will outlive you!

3. Before every trip, tighten all the bolts that secure the seats and thwarts of your canoe. Canoes naturally flex as they are paddled, hardware works loose, and cracks develop in the wood trim. Loose bolts are the major reason why seat frames and carrying yokes break on canoe trips!

OUTFITTING THE CANOE

Carrying Yoke (figure 6-2)

The rugged nature of the Boundary Waters demands that a canoe be portaged by *one* person. Two person carries are often very painful. That's because when one person climbs up on a rock, the other steps down. The result is a series of shocking blows to the shoulders and spine of both partners.

Finished pad

New England Yoke can be painful

Bolts, not screws

Staple fabric to wood block

Fabric Foam

Drainage Holes in bottom of pad

Figure 6-2

7¼'

2"

8"

2"

4"

⅛

MINNESOTA YOKE

Wood clamps for quick removal – or bolt to gunwale

It follows that your first order of business is to install a comfortable carrying yoke in the center of your canoe. The Minnesota style yoke, which consists of a curved ash thwart and two thick, foam-filled shoulder pads is, by far, the best. The contoured pads of some New England style yokes tend to gouge your shoulders when going up and down steep hills.

Boundary Waters outfitters all equip their canoes with Minnesota style yokes, though most aren't very good. Either the pads are too thin or they're spaced wrong for your shoulders. Occasionally, the yoke bar is mounted incorrectly, which makes for an unbalanced canoe that you'll have to carry over the portages! For this reason, you may want to make a custom-fitted yoke like the one illustrated in figure 6-2. Routed slots and gunnel clamps enable you to quickly install the yoke in any canoe or remove it to provide space for bulky gear or a passenger. Indeed, a quickly removable yoke is luxury you won't want to be without if you travel with three people in your canoe!

You can buy "Minnesota yokes" or curved ash bars from any mid-western canoe shop, or saw a facsimile from a straight-grained *ash* board. You'll be miserable on long portages if the yoke pads aren't spaced to match the width of your shoulders. Small-framed adults should follow the dimensions suggested for teenagers. Factory yoke pads generally measure seven inches by three inches. The suggested four by eight pads are *much more* comfortable!

Tip: If you're renting a canoe, bring along an adjustable wrench and screwdriver (slotted and Phillips) so you can unbolt the punishing metal yoke and install your own flexible wooden one!

KEEP A READY LINE ON YOUR CANOE!

Attach ten feet of quarter inch polypropylene rope (it floats) to each end of your canoe. Coil the ropes and secure them under bands of shock-cord strung through holes on the decks, or bind them with heavy rubber bands so they won't stream out when you portage. An unexpected wind can turn your beached canoe into a kite, so be sure to tie the craft to a tree whenever you go ashore!

TETHER SMALL ITEMS TO CANOE THWARTS

Drill holes through the thwarts and install lengths of elastic shock-cord through the holes. Maps and oddities placed under the elastic bands will stay put in wind and when you portage. Duct tape shock-cord to the thwarts on rental canoes.

THWART BAG(S)

Some paddlers place small items like bug dope, sun-screen and munchies in a small day pack. I prefer the handiness of a zippered bag which hangs from a canoe thwart or gunnel. You can buy commercial thwart bags, or make your own by sewing fasteners onto any fanny pack or light nylon brief case.

SEAT PADS

On a cold, blustery day, you'll wish for a warm seat pad, in camp and in the canoe. This is especially true in canoes that have temperature-sensitive aluminum seats which turn your pants gun metal gray. You can buy commercial seat pads or make your own by covering closed cell foam with *breathable* nylon or canvas. Nylon straps and Fastex™ buckles secure the pads to the seats. Or, simply duct tape closed cell foam directly to each seat.

SPONGE

If you want to keep the bottom of your canoe looking nice, you'll bring a giant sponge! Of course, you can occasionally capsize and wash your empty canoe, but I don't recommend it. The yoke pads soak up water, stay wet for days, and leak foul smelling liquid down your back when you portage.

Figure 6-1 shows a clever place to store your sponge.

LIFE JACKETS

Federal and Minnesota law *requires* canoeists to have a Coast Guard approved life vest in their canoe. You can follow the "letter of the law," or you can do what's smart—*wear your life jacket at all times while paddling!* Admittedly, everyone cheats on hot, calm days. But the rules make sense, and I urge you to stick by them. You will, if you choose a trim-fitting life vest that's cool and comfortable to wear.

PADDLES (figure 6-3)

You need a lightweight paddle for making time on the big lakes, and a more durable spare for beating about rocky shallows. Serious canoeists usually choose a relatively short, fourteen degree "bent" paddle for fast cruising, and a somewhat longer, straight paddle for rock dodging and maneuvering in tight areas.

Fifty-four inches is the most popular length for a bent shaft paddle that will be used in the typical Boundary Waters cruising canoe. This length is short enough for high cadence stroking and long enough for leverage in the turns.

Your straight paddle should be about two inches longer than your bent paddle. Long torsos and high seats require slightly longer paddles; short torsos and low seats suggest shorter paddles. Scientific formulas aside, a 54" bent-shaft and 56" straight paddle will get you around in fine style. Wide, sharp-cornered paddle blades are noisy and difficult to control, so choose a blade that is seven to eight inches wide (no wider!) and has well-rounded corners. If you prefer a very quiet paddle for fishing and approaching wildlife, consider a traditional "beavertail."

Figure 6-3

Bent Paddle   Beavertail
Paddle

CHAPTER SEVEN

Paddling and Portaging Your Canoe

PADDLING YOUR CANOE

If you can stroke forward and back and know how to "rudder," you can probably get around okay in the Boundary Waters. However, a knowledge of basic strokes will make your canoe trip much more enjoyable[1]

BIG WATER TACTICS (figure 7-1)

Loading the Canoe

Most canoes handle better when loaded *dead level.* If an uneven distribution of weight is unavoidable, the lesser of two evils is to slightly lighten the bow. But a light bow will tend to weather-vane around in a head wind, making it difficult to keep the canoe on an upwind course. On the other hand, a weighted stern will provide better directional control in a following sea, though if the tail is too low, huge waves may pour in!

Unfortunately, re-trimming your canoe to meet the changing whims of nature is practical only if there's room in the craft to move gear around. If there's not—and there won't be if you're carrying a passenger or are heavily packed for a long trip—you'd best adopt a "level trim" attitude and make the best of it. Be sure to keep the weight close to the center and low in the canoe.

When a canoe is paddled hard, the bow rises and the stern sinks into the hollow created by the wake, effectively knocking the boat out of trim, and slowing its speed. The solution is to re-trim the canoe by shifting the weight of the paddlers or cargo forward—simple enough, if the craft has a sliding bow seat (essential on a serious Boundary Waters cruiser!), or packs that can be shoved ahead.

---

[1]See my book, CANOEING & CAMPING, (ICS Books, 1992) for detailed paddle strokes and maneuvers.

Figure 7-1

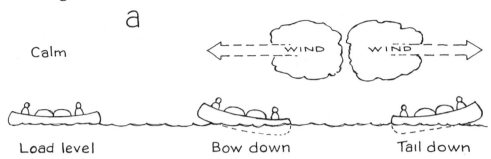

a

Calm

WIND   WIND

Load level   Bow down   Tail down

Tip: To check trim, pour some water into the canoe and
see which way it flows

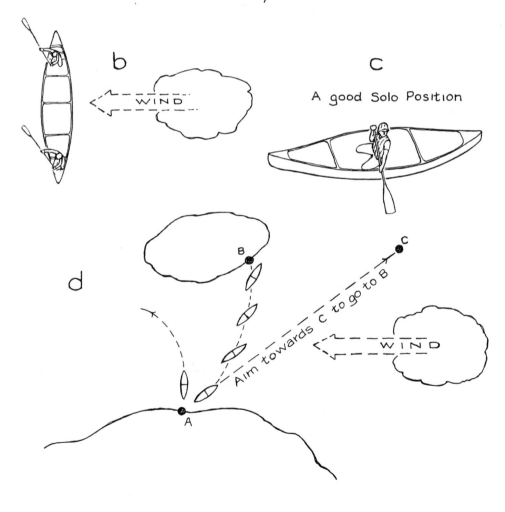

b

WIND

c

A good Solo Position

d

B

C

Aim towards c to go to B

WIND

A

With these thoughts in mind, let's review the "trim rules."

TRIM RULES

- Trim the canoe dead level for casual cruising. Keep gear centered and low in the canoe.
- Trim the canoe slightly (one inch is enough) stern down in a strong tail wind.
- Trim the canoe slightly bow down when paddling into a strong head wind. Be aware that you may have to lighten both ends of the canoe and revert to level trim if the waves are so large they come in over the bow or stern!
- Trim the canoe slightly bow down for racing. Remember, when you push a canoe hard, the bow rises and the stern falls into the trough created by the wake.

Some paddlers glue a small "fish-eye" bubble level into the hull so they can see at a glance how their boat is running. But, it's easier to pour a cup of water into the boat and observe the flow. It should pool below the center thwart for casual cruising, a bit forward when you want to make time. Keep your eye on the puddle as you paddle and you'll learn a lot about the effects of hull speed on trim.

POSITIONS FOR RUNNING UPWIND AND DOWN

On the seat or on your knees, buttocks planted firmly against the leading edge of the seat frame, is the rule, in both tandem and solo canoes. The exception is when the lake "stands on edge"!

Scenario: You're a quarter mile from shore when suddenly, the wind blows up on the big lake. You point the bow upwind and paddle for dear life. Three hundred yards ahead is an island refuge. As you pour on the coal, waves pour determinedly over the bow. What to do? If the stern paddler stays put and the bow paddler moves behind the front seat, the bow will be lightened and the craft will rise more easily to the waves. However, the heavy stern may cause the craft to weather-vane, broach and capsize.

Solution: The stern paddler shuffles forward, chest touching the stern thwart. He/she holds the paddle in a tight, deep rudder position then commands the bow person to quickly move back behind the front seat. The weight shift lightens *both* ends of the canoe, and allows the craft to "teeter-totter" over the waves. *Dead level* trim is restored so there is no loss of directional control.

Some canoeing experts advise paddlers to stay in their original positions on their seats or knees and simply "quarter" big waves at approximately a 30 degree angle as the bow beats upwind. This procedure shortens the canoe's waterline and makes it easier for the craft to fit between waves. The result is that the canoe runs drier and rises more easily to the waves.

However, a canoe on a quartering tack is constantly on the edge of broaching to the wind. The stern paddler must have complete control of the craft. An error and over you go! That's why quartering waves is best reserved for experts. Beginners are best advised to move closer amidships, as suggested above, and *paddle head on into the wind!*

Going *downwind* in a light wind is great fun, more so if you scroll a small tarp around two paddles and use it as a makeshift sail. The problem surfaces when the wind becomes strong and the canoe begins to surf. If the craft stalls on the crest of a wave, get set to swim! When suddenly the canoe feels lightheaded, act fast. The bow person should pour on the coal while the stern paddler holds a tight, deep rudder. Seconds later, the wave will pass and the canoe will slide into the trough of a smaller, more manageable wave. Now, "give 'er the ash" and get to shore before the scenario is repeated!

PADDLING ON THE SAME SIDE

Canoeing texts are usually adamant that partners should never paddle on the same side of the canoe. Hogwash! Paddling on the same side— *in unison*—is the right medicine when you can't hold the canoe on course in a quartering or side-wind. Stroke together, stay centered on your seats (or kneel!) and you won't capsize. If the wind grows too strong for this tactic, the bow person should paddle *hard* while the stern person alternately paddles and rudders.

PADDLING ALONE

Tandem canoes are generally too big to be competently handled alone. If you're serious about "soloing," you'll want a properly sized, pure-bred solo canoe. My book, *The Basic Essentials of Solo Canoeing* will get you started.

If you insist on soloing a tandem canoe on calm water, *kneel* at, or just behind the yoke (you'll want knee pads!). Move a foot or two forward (bow trimmed slightly down) when paddling into a head wind. Kneel behind the yoke when running before a breeze.

Most tandem canoes are too wide at the center to allow a comfortable paddling stroke, so you may want to scoot sideways and place both knees close together in the bilge of the canoe. This "Canadian" position is very comfortable on quiet water, though it necessarily requires that you paddle on just one side.

All other "solo techniques"—paddling backwards from the bow seat, or stroking in the stern with the bow weighted, are inefficient and, to a greater or lesser extent, downright dangerous!

CANOEING WITH A PASSENGER

One hundred fifty pounds of potatoes is a gentler, more predictable load than an equivalent weight of human cargo. Heavy packs don't move around in canoes! Passengers do, and as such, they don't exactly enhance the canoeing experience. Place a third adult or two small children in the belly of your canoe and it will ride lower, paddle harder, turn more slowly and suffer more damage when you hit rocks. Loading and unloading gear will also take on new dimensions as you stall on shallow rocks or muck yards from the portage landing. On a happy note, three adults probably won't need to make a second trip over the portages!

Where to put your passenger(s) and gear is a problem. After years of tripping with small children and teenagers, I've come to prefer this arrangement:

FOR AN ADULT OR TEENAGE PASSENGER (figure 7-2)

1. Set a large pack against the stern thwart to provide a soft backrest for your passenger. If the pack is very tall, place it on its side so it won't raise the center-of-gravity of the canoe too high.
2. Your passenger's legs could be pinned between packs and the yoke bar if the canoe capsizes. For this reason—and your passenger's comfort—you should remove the yoke from the canoe. Figure 6-2 shows one way to make a quickly detachable carrying yoke.
3. Additional packs are best placed side by side just behind the bow thwart. A thick "boat cushion" (life preserver) will keep your passenger's duff out of the accumulated bilge water. Generally, it's best if your passenger *does not* help paddle the canoe. Movable cargo, remember? The exception is when grinding into a steady head wind, where every stroke counts!

Figure 7-2

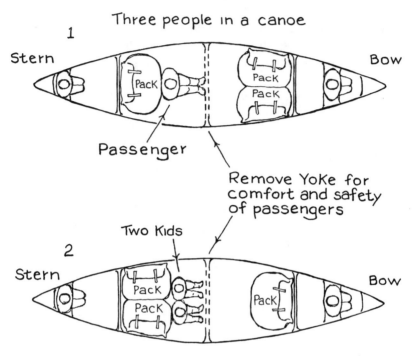

Three people in a canoe

1

Stern   Bow

Pack   Pack   Pack

Passenger

Remove Yoke for comfort and safety of passengers

Two Kids

2

Stern   Bow

Pack   Pack   Pack

Plan A - Two adults and two children

Kid one   Kid two

3

Stern   Bow

Pack   Pack   Pack

Plan B - Two adults and two children

CARRYING SMALL CHILDREN

Same procedure as above, except substitute a generously sized closed-cell foam sleeping pad for the boat cushion. If you have two small children, you have a problem: Place them side-by-side and they'll fight constantly. Separate them—one forward, one behind the yoke—and there's no place to put gear. Figure 7-2 shows some less than perfect arrangements.

TACKING (figure 7-1)

You're located at (a) on figure 7-1. There's a great campsite at (b). Head towards it and the wind will blow you past your objective. What to do? *Answer:* Aim towards (c) and the wind will take you where you want to go. One Boundary Waters canoe trip will make you a "master tacker!"

PORTAGING YOUR CANOE (figure 7-3)

Some people find that the hardest part about portaging a canoe is lifting it onto their shoulders. After years of canoeing with teenagers, I've come to prefer this energy-saving method:

Procedure: Both partners stand together on the left (port) side of the canoe, as illustrated in figure 7-3. The "portager" stands *forward* of the yoke; his or her helper stands behind it.

1. Together, the partners raise the canoe on its side.
2. Both partners grasp the yoke and pull the canoe to their thighs(a).
3. Next, they transfer their left hand to the far (right) gunnel.
   Then, they transfer their right hand to the near gunnel. Note that both of the portager's hands are forward of the yoke, while the helper's hands are behind it (b).
4. On signal, the canoe is raised overhead. The helper gets out of the way as the craft settles on to the portager's shoulders(c-d). Setting the canoe down is the reverse of picking it up.

Figure 7-3 a-b

Portager   Helper

If you canoe alone, you'll want to learn the "one person pick-up."It is identical to the "two person" method, except that the portager stands at the center (yoke) of the canoe and, in step 4 above, his or her right hand grasps the near (left) gunnel just *behind* the yoke.

There is also the classic "end" lift, in which the canoe is rolled on end and raised overhead. *Don't* use this method: It grinds the end of the canoe into the ground!

c

Figure 7-3 c-d

d

Helper leaves when canoe
is on portager's shoulders

OVER THE PORTAGE AND THROUGH THE WOODS!

Once at the portage the fun begins. All your packs, paddles, life jackets and sundries will have to be carried overland to the next lake. If you pack in *odd* units (one pack or three—never two or four) and follow this procedure, things will go much smoother.

1. Land the canoe parallel to shore if the topography permits.
2. One person holds the canoe while the other quickly strips it of gear. As soon as the craft is emptied, it is drawn up on land and placed well away from the traffic zone of the portage trail.
3. Each partner shoulders a pack and grabs a canoe paddle. Life vests are nested "coat-like" over packs, zipped around canoe thwarts, or shoved under pack flaps. Paddles, cameras and binoculars are the only items that should be hand carried. Everything else should be secured inside a pack, or "stacked" and carried with the aid of a tumpline, as suggested in the next chapter!

If you and your partner have just one pack between you, the portage may be completed in a single carry. Two trips will be needed if you have three packs. First trip over the portage, each person carries a pack and paddle. The canoe and remaining pack are brought over on the second run. The canoe is the heaviest load, so you may want to carry it first—a good idea only if you *know the trail by heart!* If you don't, you'd best bring the packs first and scout the way. Forest Service workers do their best to keep portages clear, but they have limited resources. Don't be surprised if you find storm-downed trees along seldom used trails. During high water times, normally impassable streams which are bypassed by portages may be easily canoeable. You won't spot deadfalls, or a shortcut to the next lake if your head is buried under the yoke of a canoe!

CHAPTER EIGHT

The Right Stuff!

Everything You Need to Know About Equipment

What you need in the way of equipment depends entirely on your traveling style. If portages are easy or nonexistent, fair game is whatever you can cram into your canoe. I've seen lawn chairs, cast iron dutch ovens and huge umbrella tents in the Boundary Waters. Once, I observed a galvanized garbage can in the belly of a canoe which, the owners proudly asserted, was a bear proof food cache!

At the other extreme, are a minority of experienced travelers who are willing to make long, grueling portages to get away from the crowd. Some of these people pack so light that they sacrifice their own safety and comfort!

For example, the typical four person tent weighs about three pounds more than a similar two person model, but it provides nearly twice the space. That's something to consider when bad weather confines you to its fabric walls! Similarly, it makes no sense to omit a compact folding saw and hand axe if you rely solely on fires for all your cooking.

With experience, comes wisdom. Paddlers who return to the Boundary Waters year after year, ultimately adopt a mature, middle-of-the-road approach—they bring exactly what they need and no more! Sixty five pounds per person (not including the canoe) is a reasonable weight for a week's load of food and camping gear. You can probably shave another ten pounds off this figure by tripling your equipment costs and using the latest high-tech gear.

Surprisingly, bulk is more important than weight. Most portages in the Boundary Waters are short, so a few additional pounds seldom matter. What does, are loose items that won't fit inside packsacks. Herein lies the first rule of packing right:

Except for life vests, cameras, fishing rods and paddles, every-thing must fit inside your packs!

Appendix 1 details what two people need for a week long stay in the Boundary Waters. Here are some things to consider as you assemble your kit.

Figure 8-1

PACKS

Until recently, canvas Duluth packs (figure 8-1) have reigned supreme in the Boundary Waters. Now, a plethora of nylon hiking packs threatens to dethrone the king. For most canoeists, it's a love, hate relationship. Either they swear by Duluth packs or they swear at them. Nonetheless, traditional Duluth models remain popular with experienced canoeists because they are rugged, practical, relatively inexpensive and easy to repair in the field. They are also as comfortable to carry as the best modern packs, *if you use a tumpline!*

Figure 8-2

TUMPLINE

Small Pack

TUMPLINES

A tumpline is a wide strap that attaches to a pack or bundle. You place this strap *just above* your forehead, lean forward into the trace, and take off down the trail. The early Voyageurs carried hundreds of pounds with this rig, often stacking bundles a yard high over their heads. You may follow the lead of these historic canoe men by placing awkward bundles, like day packs, paddles and fishing rods, under the tump strap in the hollow of your back, as illustrated in figure 8-2. When your neck and head begin to ache, cast off the tumpline and shift the load to the shoulder straps. Change back to the headstrap when the pain is gone.

The key to comfortable packing is *keeping the load tight against your back*—easy enough when you're hiking on the flats or downhill. But ascend a steep grade and gravity will tear at your pack and threaten to bowl you over backwards. Contoured pack frames and padded hip belts help stabilize the load, but only a tumpline anchors it tight against your back. The advantages of a tumpline on uphill grades are so pronounced that I urge you to try this simple experiment (figure 8-3):

Carry a heavy backpack up a steep staircase using the shoulder straps alone, then add a makeshift tumpline and repeat the procedure. Be sure you attach the tumpline *below* the point where the shoulder straps are sewn to the pack. You'll have to slightly loosen the shoulder straps to transfer the weight of the pack to the tumpline.

Important: Take time to adjust the tumpline right! What works for one Voyageur is wrong for another. Consider this before you give up on the grand idea.

DOUBLE-PACKING

You're half way through a two week canoe trip and one of your heavy food packs is nearly exhausted. With judicious re-packing, you can pare the load to just two packs. Your partner says he's willing to haul them both at once, if you'll manage the canoe. The payoff is that you won't have to make two trips over every portage. Should you buy the proposition?

Admittedly, you will save time by double-packing. But unless you're an old hand at it, you can trip and fall. The safest way to double-pack is to "stack load" with the aid of a tumpline, as explained above. The dangerous alternative is to sling the extra pack across your chest, which obscures your feet and the trail ahead. Step wrong, and you may twist an ankle; trip, and you could break a leg!

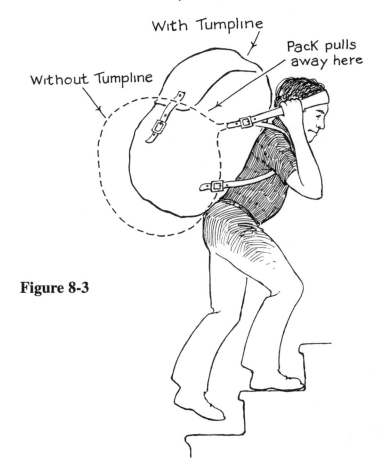

TRY THIS EXPERIMENT
Go up stairs with and without a Tumpline for your pack

With Tumpline

Pack pulls away here

Without Tumpline

Figure 8-3

I know Boundary Waters canoeists who have chest-packed for years without a single mishap. Others I know have been less fortunate. Indeed, turned ankles—which often result from double-packing—are the most common of all canoe country injuries!

Years ago, I asked my friend, Bob Dannert to define a canoeing "expert." *"Details!,"* said Bob. Small details like watching every step you take, often spell the difference between a grand experience, and a hurt you'll nurse for weeks.

Rule: If you must double-pack, "back-stack" your load, and use a tumpline. Only on the weeniest of portages should you carry a pack on your chest!

The alternative to double-packing, or making multiple trips over every portage is to stow everything in two packs—one heavy, one light. One partner carries the heavy pack, paddles, cameras, fishing gear and PFD's (whew!), while the other brings the light pack and canoe. Another option is to place everything inside a single giant pack, like the huge #4 Duluth (28" x 30" x 6"). However, big packs are awkward to handle, and they don't stow well in a canoe. Either you lay them face down in soaking bilge water or you stand them precariously high against a thwart. Load an oversize pack into a tippy canoe while you're balanced on a slippery rock, and you'll discover still another disadvantage.

Single carries are for Supermen and Wonderwomen! Mere mortals should keep pack weights and sizes reasonable. My advice? Select *three* moderately sized packs and place no more than 50 pounds of gear in each. Then, adopt a hardened attitude that "what doesn't fit, doesn't go!"

MODERN CANOE PACKS

Modern packs that have spinal-contoured shapes, padded hip belts and adjustable side-walls, are a grand alternative to traditional Duluth styles. Indeed, sophisticated backpacks are almost essential if you carry heavy loads without the aid of a tumpline. Internal frames, hip belts and other state-of-the-art backpacking features mimic, but don't equal, the performance of tumplines on uphill grades, though they do provide greater control and comfort on the flats. GRADE VI, GRANITE GEAR, and CAMP TRAILS (addresses in appendix 2) all offer great packs for serious canoeists.

Before you commit to any pack, consider these points:

1. Portaging a quarter mile, three to six times a day (the typical BWCA scenario), is not the same as hiking fifteen miles along a mountain trail. You don't need serious hiking gear for short carries. You do need equipment that stacks well in canoes!

2. Sophisticated packs offer little advantage over conventional Duluth packs, if you use a tumpline. A tumpline transfers the weight of the pack to your strong neck muscles, which negates the value of hip belts, frames and contoured shoulder straps. Tumplines also permit you to stack loose gear that won't fit inside your pack. Though, "stacking" produces an awkward load which is unsuitable for serious hiking, it speeds progress on the short portages that characterize the Boundary Waters.

3. Sophisticated features don't come cheap. State-of-the-art back packs cost nearly twice as much as traditional Duluth packs. A serious backpacker needs just one pack; a Boundary Waters canoeist needs three per canoe!

4. After a rain or capsize, you may have some wet, bulky gear that won't fit inside your pack. There's always room to "stuff one more thing" under the serviceably long closing flap of a classic Duluth pack.

5. The recommended number three size (24" x 30") Duluth pack sits upright in the canoe, pack mouth out-of-contact with bilge water. To load the pack into the canoe, you grab the pack by its "ears" (figure 8-4) and, with a deft motion, swing it over the gunnels and plop it on the floor—no bending or stooping required.

   Conversely, a long silhouette modern pack is too high to sit upright in a canoe. It must be placed belly down or side-ways (pack mouth in bilge water) in the craft. This requires considerable bending and stooping—a scenario that may be repeated dozens of times a day.

6. There's value in diversity. Why not have one Duluth pack, one modern pack, and a hard-shelled wanigan (dry box) for objects which may gouge your back? Naturally, I urge you to equip all your packs with tumplines.

Figure 8-4

Lift pack by the "ears", not the straps

and set into canoe

SHOULD YOU EQUIP YOUR PACK WITH A HIP BELT?

All the best hiking packs have padded hip belts which transfer part of the weight from your shoulders to your hips. Hip belts increase control on the flats and downhill grades, but they don't help on inclines. Hip belts also interfere with anything (sheath knife, multi-pliers, etc.) you wear around your waist.

Hip belts don't fare well in canoes. They catch on thwarts and seats during loading operations and they remain submerged in bilge water and muck for long periods of time. Each time you portage you clip the dirty, dank strap around your waist. Whenever you set the pack down on a rotting cedar or the sharp granite of the Canadian shield, abrasion takes its toll. Eventually, the padding wears through.

Nonetheless, a hip belt is a decided advantage on long, grueling portages. By alternating between shoulder straps, hip belt and tumpline, you can carry very heavy loads comfortably over difficult terrain. For this reason, some canoeists equip their modern packs with hip belts *and* tumplines.

RIGID PACKS

You'll want some sort of rigid dry box to store hard items like stove, food and cooking gear that might gouge your back. Many BWCA outfitters supply large plastic or aluminum pack boxes (wanigans) which have straps for portaging. Two strong plastic wanigans which I can heartily recommend are, the *Wanigan Canoe Pack & Pantry* (formerly, the "E.M. Wanigan")—available from Stormy Bay Enterprises, and the heavy duty polyethylene "York Pack." The addresses of these manufacturers are in appendix 2.

Here are some other rigid containers you may want to consider:

1. Purchase a woven ash pack basket from L.L. Bean or Duluth Tent, Inc. Set the basket inside a waterproof plastic bag and nest this combo in a soft pack. Secure the mouth of the plastic bag with a loop of shock-cord and you'll have a watertight seal. Duluth Tent, Inc. makes a special "Cruiser Combo" packsack which accepts a standard eighteen inch high packbasket.

2. Substitute a rectangular plastic trash can for the woven ash pack basket. You must cut off the rim of the can or it will gouge your back.

3. Follow the lead of Canadian canoeists and place hard items in plastic olive jars or plastic barrels. Three or four 15 inch diameter olive jars will fit in a #3 Duluth pack. Two foot

high plastic barrels can be purchased from western rafting companies. Marginally comfortable carrying harnesses are available from some Canadian outfitters.

4. Use a heavily varnished cardboard box instead of a pack basket or trash can. Duluth Tent, Inc. continues to make their "Standard food pack" which accepts a traditional 24 bottle beer carton.

WATERPROOF THE CONTENTS OF YOUR PACKS!

Your pack must be able to withstand an all day rain or capsize. This procedure will make any soft pack waterproof:

1. Insert a heavy (I recommend 6 mil) plastic bag into the pack. The bag should be nearly twice the length of the packsack to ensure a proper seal. This is the waterproof liner.
   You can mail order 60" X 36" plastic bags from Viking Safety Products, 710 Raymond Ave., St. Paul, MN 55114 (phone: 1-800-328-6505). These giant 6 mil bags are designed for asbestos removal and are very inexpensive.
2. Nest a sturdy fabric bag (a second 6 mil plastic bag will do) inside the waterproof liner. This abrasion liner won't tear when you stuff gear into the pack. Note that the delicate waterproof liner is protectively sandwiched between two layers of tough material—the outside pack fabric and the inside abrasion liner. Use this "sandwich method" to protect everything you want to keep dry.

For example, to waterproof your sleeping bag, first stuff it into a nylon sack, which need not be waterproof. Then place this unit inside a strong plastic bag (*the waterproof liner*). Twist, fold over, and secure the waterproof liner with a loop of shock-cord, then set the sealed bag into a slightly larger nylon stuff sack to protect it from abrasion.

TENT

It rains a lot in the Boundary Waters so you better have a tent that keeps you dry! To check the foul weather performance of any tent, pitch it on level ground and examine the fit of the rainfly (the sheet of waterproof nylon which covers the canopy). The fly should—indeed must (!)—cover *every seam and zipper!* Exposed zippers or stitching *will* leak in prolonged rain no matter how well you seal them with glue (seam-sealant).

It won't take you long to discover that simple A-frame tents rank best in deterring rain, while domes, tipis, and other geometrically sophisticated tents that have multi-seamed floors and sidewalls, rank worst. And vestibules (alcoves), which allow space to store boots and wet gear, are worth the price in any weather. Tents like the popular Eureka! timberline, which are relatively "self-supporting" set up more easily on rock than traditional "U stake-'em" models.

Always use a plastic groundcloth *inside* your tent. The ground-sheet will prevent pooled surface water which wicks through floor seams and worn floor fabric from soaking your sleeping bag. *Do not* place the plastic sheet under the tent as advised by some tent makers—rain water may become trapped between it and the floor and be pressure-wicked by body weight into the sleeping compartment!

COOKING TARP

Scenario: It's supper time and raining heavily when you pull into camp. First order of business is to set up the tents and get out of the weather. If the rain persists you'll skip supper and munch on granola bars. A hot meal can wait till morning. Right? Dead wrong!

Let's re-program the scenario to read: It's supper time and raining heavily when you pull into camp. First order of business is to erect the large rain tarp and get out of the weather. If possible, face the tarp towards your campfire, then formulate your battle plan. If you have a crew of four, two can pitch tents while one tends the fire and helps with supper. In no time, there will be soup and a cheery, protected place to share the joys of the day.

If you customize your tarp by adding extra loops and ties, as illustrated in my book *Canoeing and Camping* (ICS Books), it will go up quick and tight on any terrain.

Tip: The larger the tarp the better! Ten feet by ten feet is the right size for two. Ten by twelve is better for four. If you have five to nine people, consider bringing two tarps! Chapter 10 suggests some slick ways to rig single and double tarps.

Please don't bring cheap plastic tarps into the Boundary Waters. They are heavy, bulky, stiff and fragile. When they tear, they are often left behind to litter the wilderness. Frankly, I think the Forest Service should outlaw them!

STOVE

Even if you prefer to cook on a campfire, you should bring a stove. Stoves simplify food preparation on rainy days, and are the only way to cook if dry conditions force the Forest Service to impose a "fire ban." Stoves which burn naptha or unleaded gasoline are *much more efficient* than those which use propane, butane or alcohol.

Gasoline is best stored in approved plastic containers or aluminum fuel bottles. Most stove problems are caused by varnishes which are released by old fuel left in stoves. So empty your stove tank (burn it dry!) after every canoe trip. Coleman™ and Blazo™ fuels are best used within six months after the cans are opened. You'll have fewer problems if you keep fuel containers full to reduce the air supply needed for oxidation.

Allow one gallon of gasoline per week for a party of four, if you do all your cooking on a trail stove.

COOKWARE

Chapter 9 details the cookware you need for canoeing the Boundary Waters.

EDGED TOOLS

You need a *thin-bladed* knife, folding saw and a hand axe. Before you discount the hand axe, consider how you'll make fire when the woods are soaked with rain and the only wood available is a few well-drenched logs which you have no way to split! Chapter 10 shows how to use this maligned tool to make fire when rains come to stay.

Knife: Cutting line, slicing meats, chopping vegetables and spreading jam and peanut butter are routine chores on canoe trips. A standard jackknife is adequate, but a thin-bladed (no more than one-eighth inch across the spine!) sheath knife, giant folder or short fillet knife is more versatile. Reach deep into the peanut butter jar with your Swiss army knife and you'll instantly discover why you want a blade that's 4-5 inches long!

Tip: Good tool steel knives sharpen more easily, take a keener edge, and are much less expensive than high quality stainless models. They won't rust if you wipe them dry after every use; occasionally slice greasy foods like cheese and salami, or rub in some vegetable oil.

CLOTHING

Wool, acrylic, polypropylene and polyester (Dacron™) pile are the recommended fabrics for cool weather; cotton is fine for mid-summer heat. Several thin garments, one layered over another, are warmer and more versatile than a single, heavy coat. Heavy wool socks, a light nylon wind-shell and a broad-brimmed hat are absolutely essential.

Summer temperatures in the BWCA can go from freezing, with wind-chills near zero, to over 100 degrees in a matter of days! Long underwear, a stocking cap and gloves are important summer attire.

RAIN GEAR

A *two-piece* coated nylon rain suit or below-the-knee "fishermen's shirt" (called a "cagoule") is essential. Size the jacket large enough to wear *over* your life vest. The pants should be wide and baggy so they'll slip easily over your boots. Pant legs should not have cuffs, zippers or elastic closures at the ankles. Zippers jam and break and they restrict ventilation. You'll find sturdy rainwear at discount stores and industrial supply centers.

HATS

I carry three hats—one for sun, one for rain, and a warm stocking cap. Your sun hat should have a broad brim or "desert neck flap" to protect your ears and neck. And speaking of sun, be sure to bring sunscreen, lip balm and moisturizing lotion for your hands. Some people who have sensitive hands wear gloves when they paddle.

FOOTWEAR

Just about every type of footwear, from leather boots and sneakers to nylon "reef-runners" and river sandals, can be seen in the Boundary Waters. And, depending on the weather and the nature of the trip, a good case can be made for every one. Indeed, the perfect shoes for canoeing have not yet been invented.

Arguments as to what shoes are best rage on, but when the smoke clears, experienced paddlers agree that the best choice is a sturdy pair of water-repellent calf-high boots for portaging, and a cool, breathable pair of lightweight shoes for camp. Here's my preference:

For portaging and hiking: L.L. Bean Maine Hunting Shoes with 12 inch high leather tops and molded rubber bottoms. "Bean boots" are best worn with sheepskin, wool felt or polyethylene insoles.

In camp, I switch to high-topped canvas sneakers. I also bring a light pair of nylon "reef runners" so I won't bruise my feet while swimming.

In late October, when the people and bugs are gone, friends and I take one last trip to the Boundary Waters. Daytime temperatures often hover around 40 degrees. At night, the mercury frequently drops into the teens. More often than not, it rains and blows bloody murder; occasionally, it snows. On October 23, 1993, we encountered an inch of snow on one of the portage trails. That same day we broke quarter-inch thick ice on a small stream that exited Cherokee Lake.

At this time of year, I wear sixteen inch high rubber boots with quarter inch thick neoprene insoles. In camp, I switch to flexible knee-high Tingley™ rubber overshoes with wool felt snowmobile liners. My wardrobe includes Thermax™ long johns, wool shirt, pile sweater and Thinsulate™ filled Gore-Tex™ gloves. I bring a down jacket for chilly evenings around the campfire. The Boundary Waters is serious business when the snow falls!

SLEEPING GEAR

What you select depends on how classy you want to travel and how much money you want to spend. At the top of the list are expensive down bags, while at the bottom are discount store "gumbo-fill" specials which are no better than paired blankets. Frankly, a set of airy acrylic blankets, sandwiched "boy scout style," makes a perfectly good summer bed. A foam pad, like the deservedly popular Thermarest™, will smooth the lumps and add considerable warmth to your sleeping system.

Tip: Make a full length cotton case for your sleeping pad. The porous material will feel good against your skin on hot sweaty nights, and it will keep the slick nylon pad from sliding around in your tent as you sleep. A cover will also keep your pad clean and protect it from punctures.

KIDS' STUFF

Most children love the Boundary Waters and the sense of freedom it brings. Kids are in awe of the beauty, the smells, the wildlife. And, the quiet! Parents often report that their children are much more cooperative afield than at home.

Many parents are reluctant to take young children to the Boundary Waters, fearing they will catch cold, drown, die of hypothermia, or be eaten alive by bears. But kids are resilient. Neither rain nor cold, nor an occasional capsize will deter them from having a good time, provided they are properly dressed and well fed.

CLOTHING

Allow kids to wear blue jeans, cotton T-shirts and cotton socks (their preference) and they will be miserable when it's cold and raining. And so will you! But dress them like little adults and your days will be filled with smiles.

Kids grow out of their clothes quickly, so it makes no sense to buy expensive outdoor clothing. On the other hand, they need the right stuff to be comfortable. What to do?

Inexpensive discount store *acrylics* are ideal for children. Acrylic garments are soft and warm, and they dry quickly after a rain. They are also tolerably cool on hot days. Choose acrylic shirts, stocking caps, gloves (the kind with the rubber dots on the palm) and sweaters.

Wool clothes may be too scratchy for some children, in which case, you may substitute acrylics. However, a tightly woven wool jacshirt is worth bringing along. Wool repels water and insulates even when it's soaking wet. Few other fabrics feel as warm on a cold, rainy day. You'll find a wealth of serviceable wool shirts at area garage sales. Cook them in hot water for a while and they'll shrink to fit!

Polypropylene and pile: Great stuff if you can find small sizes and good prices. Heat severely shrinks polypropylene and pile, and you can use this to your advantage to provide a custom fit. **Caution:** Use hot water, not your clothes drier to shrink fit these garments. High drier heat may *melt* polypropylene!

RAIN GEAR

The most practical and least expensive rain gear for children is a cut-to-fit plastic poncho, a standard rain coat and a sou'wester hat with lined ear-flaps. Here's the rationale: The youngster sits on a boat cushion in the middle of the canoe and wears all three garments. Arms that poke through the poncho sides stay dry, and the two-layer construction provides extra protection against blowing rain. The long draping sides of the poncho keep crossed legs and feet dry, while the sou'wester hat discourages dribbles at the neck. The outfit provides good ventilation when portaging.

FOOTWEAR

High topped canvas basket ball shoes are ideal for warm, dry days. Slip on inexpensive Tingley™ rubber boots when rains come to stay. *Two* pairs of socks should always be worn inside shoes. The thin, inner pair may be polypropylene, acrylic or Thermax™, the outer pair, nearly pure wool. The main reason for doubled socks is to prevent heat blisters, not to increase warmth. Inner socks should be worn *inside out*, so that blister-causing seams will be away from the skin.

SLEEPING BAGS AND KIDDY PADS

A small acrylic blanket is adequate for summer travel in the Boundary Waters. The blanket will wash easily and dry quickly if your child has an "accident" while sleeping. Bring some diaper pins so you can convert the blanket to a sleeping bag on chilly nights. To this, add a closed cell foam pad (carpet padding will suffice) for warmth below, and your child is set for the sandman.

TOYS AND ENTERTAINMENT

Be sure to provide a downsized paddle and a small day pack for your little passenger. A favorite stuffed animal is sure to go along, so be sure to provide a "rain coat" (plastic poly bag) for it. Granola and home made cookies are wholesome between-meal snacks, and they have no wrappers to pollute the environment—a concern when traveling with children who, unthinkingly throw things about.

PACKING YOUR PACKS

Follow this procedure and you'll never have to eat damp oatmeal!

Distribute your food among several packs. This equalizes weight and provides a backup in the event you lose a pack to a hungry bear (more on this in chapter 10). Double-seal your food in plastic, as suggested in chapter 9, and place meals on the *bottom* one-fourth of each pack. Pack everything in *horizontal* layers so the back of your pack sack will follow the curve of your spine. You may want to pack things in this order:

First, set your sleeping bag on the bottom of your pack, on top of the food packets.

Your foam sleeping pad goes next, followed by your clothes, which are contained in a pillow-case size, nylon stuff sack. Put your remaining sundries on top of your clothes bag.

Now, roll down and seal the inner abrasion liner. The tent goes on top. It should fit snugly, like a cork in a bottle. Stakes and poles are best packed in a *separate* bag!

When you're satisfied with the arrangement, roll down and *seal* the outer, waterproof pack liner. Place your rain gear and tent pole bag on top. Sew nylon loops to the pole bag ends and run the closing straps of the packflap through the loops so poles won't slide out from under the packflap.

Note that everything is contained and watertight. The tent, which may be wet or damp, is protected from a capsize, and is isolated from your dry clothing and sleeping gear. Long tent poles that won't fit crossways in your pack won't head for the deep six if you capsize.

In camp, unpacking is easy. Rain gear, tent and poles are right on top of your pack, followed by sundries, clothes and sleeping gear. Food stays put until you need it.

PACKING THE CANOE

Adopt a standard procedure for packing and unpacking your canoe. Your system should be geared for speed and "level trim." Figure 8-5 shows some common packing layouts.

Things to remember: Locate packs so that rain gear, nylon windshell, gloves and sweater are handy. Your canoe will rise to the waves more easily if you keep weight close to the center of the canoe. Don't "string out" gear or pile it high above the gunnels.

Figure 8-5

a

Rear
Seat

b

c

Thwart

Some common packing layouts

Fast Fixin's

Easy Ways to Prepare Great Trail Meals!

In 1967, a friend and I loaded my then-new Sawyer Cruiser canoe atop his station wagon and headed north to Grand Marais, Minnesota—gateway to the Boundary Waters Canoe Area. Our trip lasted ten days and traversed 100 miles—fairly substantial for first-timers. We began on Seagull lake, swung north almost to Ely, then followed the Canadian border east to Trail's End landing on Saganaga Lake. By today's standards, we were marginally prepared. Our primitive single-walled nylon tent leaked in the sporadic rains, our little Sawyer canoe swamped in waves, and our bland but nutritious meals took too long to prepare. Nonetheless, we had a marvelous time.

Other than instant soups and the famed Boy Scout trail packs, dried foods were largely a novelty in the 1960's. It took know-how and experience to assemble well-balanced, lightweight meals, so my friend and I decided that it would be best if an experienced outfitter supplied our food. Both of us were serious coffee drinkers, and we strongly noted this on the menu request form.

"No problem," assured our outfitter. "It'll all be packed and waiting when you arrive at our base in Grand Marais."

Disappointment reared its head at supper time the first night out, when we discovered that one pint of ground coffee would have to last ten days. My friend was even more furious when he learned that there was no cream or sugar. In place of what we needed were things we didn't want—white bread for sandwiches and French toast, hot chocolate and instant pistachio pudding. We vowed that next year, we'd leave the food planning to us!

Dried foods have come a long way since the 1960's. Now, you can get almost anything from cholesterol-free egg substitutes to sour cream at big league supermarkets and cooperatives. What you can't find in local stores, you can mail order from specialty houses. Hamburger, beans, beef jerky and other staples may be easily dehydrated and vacuum sealed (more on this later) at home. And if this seems like too much work, canoe outfitters will wow you with a variety of delicious freeze-dried offerings, which range from fillet mignon to lobster biscayne.

However, there's smug satisfaction in self-sufficiency. If you love good food, you'll want to provide for your own tastes. Here's how to prepare gourmet meals without a lot of work.

HARDWARE

For a party of four, you'll need one 10-inch diameter, Teflon-coated skillet with cover, two *nesting* pots with covers, and a twelve cup coffee pot or teakettle. The largest pot should have a 16 cup capacity so you can cook pasta without gluing it to the bottom. Pots may be aluminum, stainless steel or porcelain-lined steel. Sustained cooking in aluminum has been linked to Alzheimer's disease—hardly a concern considering the minimal use received by most camp cookware.

You'll be cooking on a trail stove or Forest Service grill so wire bail handles are not essential. One long pot handle or two protruding metal "ears" per pot, are adequate if you have insulated pot holders—gloves, bandannas or pliers. Discount store kitchenware often works better than expensive pots and pans which are designed for camping. This is especially true for skillets.

I purchase a high grade Teflon™ lined skillet and replace the Bakelite™ handle with a quickly removable one which I bend from 0.187 inch diameter spring wire (see figure 9-1). The mounting bracket for the handle is made from hardware store aluminum flat stock. It secures with two brass bolts which are easily detached when the pan wears out. I also outfit some of my pots with these rigid wire handles.

Tips: Engrave lines on the pot sides at two cup intervals and write the total capacity (e.g. 16 cups) just below the rim. This will eliminate guesswork and the need for measuring cups at meal time. For faster heating, you may want to blacken the bottoms of your aluminum pots. Alumablack™—a chemical used for blackening aluminum hardware on firearms—is ideal for this purpose. Every gun shop has it.

A wide-based teakettle heats faster and is less tippy than a coffee pot, and it permits you to pour with one hand. Pack fresh onions, green peppers and other crushables inside your empty teakettle (see Meal Management Tricks on page 85).

You may also want an oven. You can buy commercial models or simply rig a "double-pan" or "dutch" oven from the cookware you already have. You can also prop a frying pan to face the fire and cook your bakestuff by reflected heat. Figure 9-2 shows the traditional procedures.

Figure 9-1

Commercial Teflon™-lined skillet

Removable brass bolt

Figure 9-2

Baking is a rather time-consuming process, one best reserved for lazy layover days. Pita, bagels, nutritious crackers and an assortment of preservative-filled cocktail breads and cakes that keep for weeks, have largely replaced the need for fresh baked goods. Nonetheless, if you enjoy baking, do it. After all, it's your canoe trip and you need to please no one but yourself!

Be sure to provide an insulated cup, sturdy plastic bowl, metal fork and spoon for each person. A stainless steel cup makes a handy ladle.

You may also want a fabric utensil roll that has snaps or ties at the top so you can hang it from a branch or overhead line. Contents should include a large wooden spoon, wire whip, rubber spatula, bamboo tongs, regulation cast aluminum Boy Scout pot gripper (these are the best!), Teflon™-proof wood or plastic pancake turner, and a removable spring steel handle for your frying pan.

Dish washing materials: A 3M nylon "scratcher", Teflon™-safe nylon sponge and a small bottle of biodegradable detergent. Pack a few sheets of paper toweling with every meal and you won't have to dry dirty cotton dish towels.

SPICES

Dried foods are generally pretty bland unless they're heavily spiced. I carry oregano, garlic powder, seasoned salt, black pepper and cayenne inside small film containers which are kept in a nylon "spice bag."

PACKING THE KITCHEN

Nest the pots and covers and place them in a generously sized fabric bag. Pack spices, dish washing materials and your Sierra cup ladle inside the smallest pot, along with the nesting plastic bowls. Forks and spoons go inside the utensil roll. Everyone carries their own drinking cup in a thwart bag or on a lanyard, tied to the canoe. The teakettle or coffee pot is usually the last thing that's packed when you break camp in the morning. For this reason—and because you may want noon-time tea or soup—it is best placed in a fabric bag and packed at the top of a pack, where you can get at it quickly.

CONTAINERS FOR POWDERS AND LIQUIDS

Sugar, flour and other powdered foods may be safely carried in sealed plastic bags which are nested inside strong nylon or cotton bags. Use plastic bottles for cooking oil, pancake syrup, jam, and other liquids. Laboratory proven Nalgene™ bottles are the most reliable field container, but they are very expensive. Hospitals and clinics routinely discard strong plastic bottles which are used to store sterile, intravenous solutions. These containers are watertight, lightweight, and nearly indestructible. And, they don't seem to hold food odors like other plastics. They come in graduated sizes from 500 to 1500 ml and have a convenient lanyard hole. Ask your doctor to save these IV bottles for you.

EASY BREAKFASTS

Instant Quaker Oats or Cream of Wheat with raisins and beef jerky is the traditional fare for fast moving days when you want to "get up and go." Here are some flavorful options which require less than twenty minutes to prepare:

CINNAMON/RICE AND GOLDEN RAISINS

When I was a kid, one of my favorite breakfasts consisted of hot milk, steamed white rice, golden raisins and cinnamon and sugar to taste. I had forgotten how good this was until a friend prepared it on a recent Boundary Waters trip. In the old days, mom simmered long grain rice in whole milk. Today, fast cooking Minute Rice™ and non-fat dry milk work as well. Kids and adults both relish this easy-to-prepare nutritious meal. Add powdered orange drink or dehydrated fruit and you'll have a balanced meal

WHEN OATMEAL GETS BORING, TRY THESE DELICIOUS HOT CEREALS!

Red River Cereal is a nutritious, blend of crunchy grains that's served in the best fishing camps in Canada. It cooks to a rich, creamy consistency in just five minutes.

Big Bill's Multi Grain Cereal is another tasty Canadian product. Sweetened malted whole milk provides unique flavor. "Bill's" can be mail ordered direct from Harvest Food Works in Smith Falls, Ontario . (see appendix 2).

Hot Ralston is another traditional alternative to oatmeal. Simmer raisins, dehydrated apples, cinnamon and brown sugar for a few minutes in the boiling water *before* you add the cereal. Ditto for Red River and Bill's multi-grain cereals.

TRICKS WITH EGGS

If space and weight are a concern, you'll want to carry freeze-dried eggs. Otherwise, fresh eggs are less expensive and tastier. Farm fresh eggs will keep for weeks without refrigeration!

Small and medium size eggs have thicker shells than large eggs, so they're less apt to break on a canoe trip. I carry fresh eggs in their original cardboard (not styrofoam!) containers. I seal each egg carton in a plastic poly bag then place it inside a strong Tupperware™ container which holds up to four dozen eggs. The Tupperware safe goes inside my pack basket or on top of my Duluth pack. I can't recall when I've ever had a spoiled or broken egg. The Tupperware box doubles as a dish pan, and as a convenient safe for other crushables when the eggs are gone.

EGG /CHEESE McPITA / McTORTILLA

Option 1: Fry and set aside two thin slices of Canadian bacon or summer sausage, per person. Scramble one egg per person and set it aside. Now, lightly fry an open face Mediterranean pocket bread (pita) or tortilla in a teaspoon of cooking oil. When the bottom of the pita or tortilla is brown (20 seconds), flip the bread over and lay thin sliced cheese on top. Pile on the bacon or sausage and egg, add a dash of your favorite salsa (optional), and immediately, toss a dash of cold water into the sizzling skillet. Cover and steam for fifteen seconds then serve *immediately.* In less than a minute you'll have a wholesome, delicious sandwich everyone will enjoy.

Option 2: Same as above, but fry the egg "over easy," or omit it. Bacon/cheese pitas/tortillas are marvelous!

Option 3: GARLIC/CHEESE PITA OR GARLIC CHEESE BURRITO.

Cut pita bread in half and fill the pockets with thin-sliced or grated cheddar, monterey jack or Swiss cheese. Heavily sprinkle garlic powder and oregano (optional) over the cheese. Fry each pita half in a *well oiled, covered* skillet for about twenty seconds. As soon as you flip the pita, add a dash of cold water to "steam the cheese."

Tortillas are less filling than pitas but they have a more delicate toasty flavor. Cook each tortilla flat in a well-oiled skillet for about ten seconds, then flip it over and add cheese and garlic powder to the toasted side. Immediately roll the tortilla into a burrito shape, add cold water to steam, then cover and simmer for twenty seconds. Mmmm, good! Serve "garlic cheese burritos" as an hors d'oeuvre with chili, pasta dishes and soup.

CINNAMON TORTILLAS, STEWED FRUIT AND CANADIAN BACON

Make a tortilla burrito as described above, but substitute margarine, cinnamon and white or brown sugar for the cheese and garlic. Tastes just like a cinnamon roll!

Boiled dehydrated apples and brown sugar, with a side of Canadian bacon round out this perfect meal.

Note: Fresh baked pita bread and tortillas will keep at least two weeks on a mid-summer canoe trip if they are well-sealed when you leave home.

LAUNCHING LUNCH

Lunches should be easy. If you can't unwrap it, spread it or slice it, forget it! Here again, pita bread becomes an important staple. Fill pitas with cheese, jam, peanut butter and hard salami. For variety, substitute flavored Rye Krisp™, Wheat Thins™ and other crackers for pita bread, and serve granola, beef jerky, meat sticks, cookies, dehydrated fruit and salted nut rolls. Lightweight Nutrasweet™ flavored drink mixes make tepid water bearable.

ON INTO SUPPER

Pork chops, stroganoff, chicken alfredo, Cajun black beans with rice, and spumoni ice cream, are all available in freeze-dried form. You can even get freeze-dried steaks, if you can find them. And, afford them!

Few campers are willing to pay the high prices that freeze-dried specialty foods command. As a result, there are fewer dried food makers today than a decade ago. The ones that survive, eke a meager profit from selling traditional entrees like "spaghetti and meatballs," "beef stroganoff" and "Denver omelets" to inexperienced outdoors people who lack the skills to produce similar meals from supermarket offerings.

Here are some things to consider as you plan your freeze-dried/dehydrated suppers.

1. Most dried entrees consist of three parts—pasta or rice, freeze-dried chicken, beef or shrimp, and spices. Remember this, and you can mix and match a variety of foods to suit your tastes.
2. The meat is by far the most expensive part of any dried meal. One quarter pound of freeze-dried hamburger (essential to make spaghetti, stroganoff or chili) costs three times as much as a Big Mac! Chicken and shrimp are even more expensive.

However, you can easily dry these meats in no time at all in an inexpensive home dehydrator. For example, here's how to dehydrate hamburger :

1. Fry the hamburger and drain the grease. I allow cooked hamburger to stand in a wire strainer for several minutes, then I pour boiling water through the meat to remove as much fat as possible.
2. Line each dehydrator tray with a few sheets of absorbent paper toweling and spread the hamburger out on the trays. Allow no more than one pound (quarter inch thickness) of hamburger per tray.
3. Turn the dehydrator to high (140°F.) and come back in 24 hours. Vacuum seal[1] (best) the dried hamburger in one-pound lots, or double-bag it in Zip-lock™ bags. Use a drinking straw to remove as much air as possible from the Zip-lock™ bags. Vacuum-sealed, dehydrated hamburger will keep at least a year at room temperature; carefully Zip-locked™ hamburger should last a month. As a safety precaution, keep dehydrated meats frozen until just before your trip.

Use dehydrated hamburger in spaghetti, chili, soups and stews.

Here's a hearty meal for four that takes just ten minutes to prepare:

HAMBURGER/CHEESE VEGETABLE SOUP

Add one pound (about three-fourths cup) of dried hamburger to eight package servings of vegetable soup. Toss in a heavy handful of wide egg noodles or instant rice, and add some dried mushrooms (optional) and a few slices of cheese. A dash of red pepper and garlic powder complete the recipe. I'm betting this will be one of your favorite meals!

[1]Several excellent vacuum sealing machines are available. I've had good luck with a powerful home unit called the FOODSAVER. It's available from Nationwide Marketing, Inc. 1550 Bryant St., Suite 850, San Francisco, CA 94103. Phone 1-800-777-5452.

To prepare spaghetti, you'll need dehydrated hamburger, pasta, spices and tomato paste. Chili requires dehydrated beans which are easily made from canned beans, as follows: Dump canned beans (pour off the bulk of the liquid) directly on the dehydrator tray and turn the heat to high. The beans will be dried and ready to pack in about eight hours.

To make the spaghetti sauce, line the dehydrator trays with plastic cling wrap and spread the sauce evenly on the trays. In twelve hours you'll have a thin, rubbery mass that resembles a fruit roll up. Peel the dried sauce off the plastic wrap, roll it up and freeze it. Later, break chunks into a plastic poly bottle. Add water to the chunks to rehydrate the sauce.

If you don't want to mess with this foolishness, simply order tomato powder at your local co-op. Add a little water to the powder and you'll get paste; add more water, and you'll have sauce or soup.

PITA PIZZA

After several days of boring one pot meals, you'll appreciate some solid food that you can chew. Everyone will love "pita pizza." Here's how to make it:

Ingredients: One or two pieces of pita bread per person, dried tomato powder, fresh mozzarella cheese (hard, fresh cheese keeps nearly a month if it's encased in wax or vacuum sealed), oregano, garlic powder, salt, cayenne pepper. Any or all of the following: Dried pepperoni, summer sausage, hard salami, Canadian bacon, fresh onion, green pepper, dried mushrooms.

Procedure:

1. Thin slice and fry the meat and drain off the grease on paper toweling. Thickly dice the vegetables, fry them in light oil, then drain off the grease and set them aside. Rehydrate the mushrooms in water for several minutes, then pour off the water, pat dry the mushrooms and lightly fry them in oil. Set the mushrooms aside along with the other vegetables.

2. To make the pizza sauce, pour a half cup of tomato powder into a bowl and add water to make a thick paste. Sprinkle on oregano, garlic, salt and cayenne. Allow the sauce to blend for a few minutes.

3. Fry an open-faced pita at low heat in a well-oiled, covered skillet. When the bottom of the pita is brown (about 20 seconds), flip over the pita and thickly spread on tomato sauce, cheese, meat and vegetables to taste. Immediately add a dash of water (to steam-melt the cheese) and cover the pan. Allow the pizza to cook at very low heat for half a minute, or until the cheese has melted.

MEAL MANAGEMENT TRICKS

Add Fresh Vegetables to all Your "One Pot" Meals!

Unrefrigerated onions, tomatoes and green peppers will keep about five days on a canoe trip, if they are "properly" packed.

Onions are so tough you can just place them in a *cotton* or *paper* bag. Stow the bag inside a rigid container, like a covered teapot, cardboard milk carton or plastic dry box.

Use this procedure for green peppers and tomatoes which spoil quickly and are easily bruised:

1. Wash the vegetables, then immerse them in a sink full of drinking water that has been treated with about one-eighth cup (the amount isn't critical) of chlorine bleach. Allow the vegetables to soak for several minutes in the treated water before you dry and pack them away. The bleach will kill the surface bacteria which promotes spoilage. A similar procedure is used in some of America's finest restaurants to keep vegetables fresh.
   You may use only a small portion of a tomato or pepper at each meal. Wash in fresh water only the portion you need. Do not wash the entire vegetable! Doing so will introduce water-borne bacteria which may precipitate spoilage.

2. Separately wrap each tomato or green pepper in clean paper toweling. Pack the towel-wrapped veggies in a paper or cotton sack and set the sack inside a crush-proof container, as suggested above. Do not wrap vegetables in non-porous plastic!

Tip: A squish-resistant, plastic "tennis ball" tube makes a good safe to store tomatoes or onions. Be sure to punch holes in the sides of the tube so air will circulate.

PACK _EVERYTHING_ YOU NEED FOR A GROUP MEAL INSIDE A COLOR-CODED NYLON STUFF SACK.

Your crew will consume twenty-one meals on a seven day canoe trip. That's a lot of food to keep track of. This procedure will simplify packing and help you identify who has what meal.

Procedure:

1. Lay out on the floor, twenty-one large poly bags in three rows of seven each. Pack each group breakfast in a separate bag in the bottom row. Lunches go in the middle row of bags, suppers in the top row.
2. Seal each plastic bag and place it in a sturdy, color-coded nylon stuff sack. I pack breakfasts in "green" sacks, lunches in "blue," and suppers in "red." Tag the contents of each stuff sack so you can identify each meal.

Say your crew decides to prepare a spaghetti supper. How can you find it among the twenty-one meal bags? Easy! Suppers are packed in "red" bags, remember? Get out the seven red bags and look for the "spaghetti" label. What could be easier?

TASTY COOKING TRICKS

Ever notice how some campers can always prepare great meals while others can't warm soup without burning it? Good camp chefs know a wealth of tasty cooking tricks. Here are a few that will speed food preparation and save stove fuel and/or firewood.

MAKE A COZY SWEATER FOR YOUR COOKING POTS!

It's a cold, blustery day and you're anxious for a hot meal. You place the pot of freeze-dried chili on your stove to heat, taking care to stir constantly so the food won't burn. You know that if you stop stirring and cover the pot, the chili will boil faster. However, it may also burn and stick to the pot bottom. On the other hand, if you continue to stir the uncovered food, heat will escape into the air and the chili will take much longer to cook. What to do?

Make an insulated sweater "cozy" for your pot from any quilted or knitted material. A two-piece cozy (top hat and pot band) like the one illustrated in figure 9-4, is more versatile and energy efficient than a one-piece model. Here's how to use your two-piece cozy.

Figure 9-4

"COZY COOKING"

Velcro secures Cozy skirt

Cozy ½ inch below edge of pot

Cozy Band deflects cold wind and keeps heat in when cover is removed

Exposed metal prevents Cozy from burning

Grab Loop

Cover Skirt

Cozy Band

Velcro

Mating Velcro

When done cooking, set hot pot on closed-cell foam pad

1. Secure the insulated band around the pot before you begin cooking. Pour cold water into the pot and add only the dehydrated hamburger and vegetables. Tightly cover the pot and Velcro™ down the cozy skirt to provide an overlapping seal. Turn the stove to high and attend to other chores.
2. When the water boils, reduce the heat to "medium" and add the chili beans, tomato powder and spices. Stir vigorously until the fixin's are blended and the water is boiling again (about thirty seconds).
3. Turn off the stove, put on the cover and cozy and set the pot on a piece of closed cell foam, a square of old carpeting or a pot holder. The chili will "slow cook" to perfection in about 20 minutes!

The advantage of the two-piece cozy over a one-piece "teapot" model is that the wide band continues to insulate the pot sides when you remove the cover to stir. The skirted "top hat" can also be used alone on top of a skillet cover to increase its thermal efficiency. It is especially useful when steam-cooking pita pizza and tortilla burritos. Your pots may be insulated with spare clothing if you don't have a fitted cozy. *Caution:* Nylon or acrylic fabrics will melt! Cotton or wool fabrics are best.

As mentioned, a dash of cold water in a hot, covered skillet will quickly steam-cook foods. You can also use this method to restore the freshness of week-old bagels, pita bread and tortillas . Simply "steam grill" the bread in a covered skillet for a few seconds.

Finally, if you insist on carrying loaves of bread, here's an old woodsman's trick that guarantees perfect toast: Distribute a heavy pinch of table salt on the surface of a hot, dry (no grease!) skillet. Set a slice of bread on the salt. *Do not* cover! When the bottom of the bread is toasted to a golden brown, flip the bread over and toast the other side. The salt won't burn or stick to the bread or skillet.

CHAPTER TEN

A Bomb-Proof Canoe Camp!

Some years ago, after a dangerous storm with winds to 50 miles an hour, a teenager and I went out to fetch water on Little Saganaga lake in the Boundary Waters Canoe Area. Everywhere, wind and rain had wreaked havoc upon the land. Clumps of uprooted vegetation floated aimlessly about and waist-thick trees were downed and scattered all around. We could see three other camps from our vantage point and there was not a tent or tarp standing in any one of them. One site revealed a thin column of smoke which suggested a barely sputtering blaze. There was not a whisper of flame in the others. A comically intricate network of ropes, pressured low by heavy piles of wet clothing was a universal phenomenon.

We filled our kettles with clean water then cruised on back to our campsite where five teenagers were busily tending to chores. Daintily strung from a line near the crackling fire was the only wet gear in camp—a red wool lumberjack shirt and some bathing suits and towels. Held firm by a web of brightly colored parachute cords (for good visibility in failing light), our two low slung rain tarps had weathered the storm without pooling water. Everything beneath them was sunshine dry.

I pulled the canoe ashore and set the huge teapot on the fire, then turned to a sandy-haired girl nearby. "You guys stay dry last night?" I asked.

"Yeah, except my wool jacket which dumbo here (pointing to her freckle-faced friend) borrowed and left out all night!"

"Don't fight, children," I teased. "We won't blow this place till noon. By then, everything will be dry. Now if you guys wanna see a show, check out our neighbors 'round the bend." "Yeah," perked the boy who had joined me in the canoe—"we got us one bomb-proof canoe camp here!"

Surprisingly, "bomb-proofing" a canoe camp against the cruelties of nature is more a function of skill than things. As the anecdote suggests, you don't have to paddle far to find inept bozos with high tech gear and no savvy. So first learn the ropes, then attend to equipment. And take these suggestions seriously:

SUGGESTION: Always use a waterproof groundcloth inside your tent! I mentioned this in the last chapter, and it's so important that it bears repeating here. The best rain tent won't keep you dry if it's pitched in a low spot—a situation you can't control on the federally designated tent sites in the Boundary Waters. Indeed, even high ground will soak through if it rains long enough and hard enough. It follows that you *absolutely, positively* must place a watertight plastic layer between your sleeping gear and the tent floor.

Check out a tent full of teenagers after a heavy rain: If there was no protective ground cloth, the kids who occupied the perimeter of the tent will be soaking wet. Those who slept in the middle will be comfortably dry and tight-lipped about the reason why!

Some canoeists place a second ground cloth under the floor of their tent to protect it from scrapes. Frankly, I think this is a bad idea. Here's why:

1. If it rains hard and long enough, water may become trapped between the exterior plastic and tent floor, and be pressure-wicked by body weight into the sleeping compartment. Using a ground cloth under the floor is akin to pitching your tent on a slab of concrete!
2. If it's storming when you pull into camp, you'll have to battle a wind-blown mass of soaking wet plastic that threatens to become airborne at any moment!
3. A second ground cloth is additional weight and bulk you don't need on a canoe trip.
4. As I suggested in the last chapter, holes more often develop from inside packs, than outside. Ditto, tent floors! The extra thickness provided by a four mil thick, interior plastic ground cloth will prevent thorns and pine cones from puncturing the nylon tent floor.

SUGGESTION: Add extra stake loops and guy points to your tent so it won't blow down in high winds.

Sew nylon "storm loops" to critical places like the center sidewall and hem. The more stake points you have along the perimeter, the tighter your tent will stay in a storm. Most tents have only three or four stakes per side; five is better!

Wherever possible, attach storm lines to the *metal framework* of the tent, not the rain fly. It's an advantage if you can Velcro™ storm loops to adjacent poles, as illustrated in figure 10-1. This transfers wind stress from the nylon fly to the metal frame. A stock Eureka! timberline tent, pitched on an exposed site and rigged with the customary eight stakes and no guylines, will often bend poles and become airborne when winds reach 25 miles per hour. Add the extra stakes and storm-lines, suggested in figure 10-1, and it may stand firm in winds of twice that speed!

SUGGESTION: Double stake your tent on soft ground; use log or rock anchors on rock. Two stakes per loop—each through a separate hole, and at a different angle—doubles the surface area and holding power in soft ground. On rock or sand, try the method illustrated in figure 10-2. *Tip:* Tie three foot lengths of parachute cord to each stake loop, *before your canoe trip*, and you won't have to mess with cutting and tying these anchor lines in a rain storm!

Figure 10-1

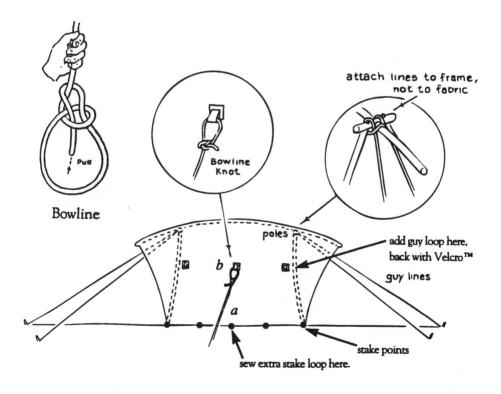

Bowline

Bowline Knot

attach lines to frame, not to fabric

poles

add guy loop here, back with Velcro™

guy lines

Pull

sew extra stake loop here.

stake points

Figure 10-2

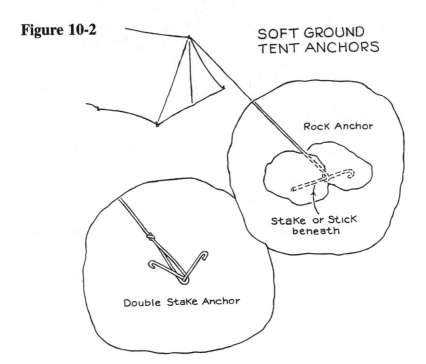

SOFT GROUND
TENT ANCHORS

Rock Anchor

Stake or Stick
beneath

Double Stake Anchor

SUGGESTION: Don't leave home without one or two customized nylon rain tarps!

One or two "customized" nylon tarps, with enough cord and stakes to rig them, will provide a dry place to cook and get out of the weather. The alternative to a tarp is to dog house it in your tent until the storm subsides.

Figure 10-3

quick-release
power cinch

power cinch

½" rope

quick-release
half-hitch

secure to
tree or stake

RIGGING TRICKS

1. The corner grommets of your tarp won't tear loose in high winds if you tie the leading edge of the tarp to a tight rope, as illustrated in figure 10-3.
2. If you carry two tarps, rig one lean-to style (open front, back staked down) and "float" the other overhead to provide a horizontal awning. If you leave a generous air space between the overlapped portions of the two tarps, smoke from a rock-backed campfire will be drawn out through the hole rather than into the shelter.

SUGGESTION: A hand axe and folding saw will simplify making fire when the woods are soaked from days of rain.

If you're tripping in the heart of Canada where dead, downed wood is everywhere, you can probably eliminate the axe. But it's a blessing if you camp on heavily used sites in the Boundary Waters where all the good wood has been picked over, and making fire means splitting logs to get at the dry heartwood inside.

Admittedly, an axe in the hands of an insensitive fool is danger-ous to flesh and vegetation—good reasons why federal authorities want to outlaw all choppers. Nonetheless, thousands of experienced campers use axes responsibly. I've always carried a hand axe on my canoe trips and have never had an "axident"—good fortune which I attribute to a rigid policy that does not allow chopping. Here's how I make fire on a rainy day.

FIRST, LOCATE DRY WOOD!

In the days before environmental concerns, birch bark torn from trees, wilted cedar foliage and dry pine needles scraped from the forest floor, were all acceptable fire-making materials. And so were dead twigs gathered from the base of conifer trees and wood robbed from beavers' dams. Now, taking these materials is unthinkable. Indeed, any activity which degrades the look of the land is ecologically unac-ceptable, if not illegal.

To find "good" firewood, locate a *dead, downed tree*, out-of-sight of tents and trails, and saw off the longest limb you can carry. Avoid wood which touches the ground, as it is apt to be rotten.

Please don't be tempted by downed wood along the lake shore or at the edge of your campsite. Your fresh cuttings will take the wildness out of the wilderness for all who follow!

Use this method to cut and split your firewood.

1. Saw the dead wood branch or bole into foot-long sections. Stand a piece on end, preferably on a heavy, split log base.
2. Gently bury the axe in the end grain and firmly grasp the handle with both hands. Now, ask your friend to pound the blade on through with a small log.

To safely split fine kindling, set the woodbe splitting upright on a log and hold it in place with a long stick. Then, come down lightly with the hatchet. If you miss your target, you won't cut yourself!

Splitting wood to get at the dry heartwood, is the most practical way to make and maintain a campfire in severe weather. Large axes are dangerous, and unnecessary. Any tool that's used for "chopping" can slip. And cut! When used as prescribed, the maligned little hand axe is a safe and efficient splitting tool.

FIRE-MAKING TIPS

1. The trunk of the balsam fir tree has resin blisters which contain highly flammable pitch. Lance a blister with a sharp stick, collect the resin and use it to start your fire. Note: Sap weepings attract insects, so please reserve this procedure for genuine emergencies!
2. Search the woods for a dead conifer stump. Roots concentrate resin (pitch) which burns violently. A few sticks of "pitch wood" will ignite wet wood and fuel a campfire for hours.
3. Cedar is the firewood of choice in the Boundary Waters. It contains volatile resins which burn violently, even when the wood is damp. Cedar cuts and splits more easily than other woods and it doesn't produce sparks which can set the woods on fire. Learn to identify this wonderful straight-grained wood with the fibrous bark.

And a plea for conscience: It won't take you long to discover that green cedar boughs burn vigorously, even when soaking wet. However, picking green foliage is unethical, illegal (there is a costly fine), and it damages the trees! As mentioned, you can easily obtain dry kindling from dead wood splittings. Fine shavings, whittled from cedar heartwood, may be the best tinder of all.

4. Carry a butane lighter, a tube of Mautz Fire Ribbon™ (a chemical fire-starter) and a large plumber's candle, and you'll have no trouble making fire in any weather!

CHAPTER ELEVEN

Bothersome Beasts and Ornery Stingers!

BOTHERSOME BEASTS

Quick! What do you think people fear most about camping in the Boundary Waters? If you said "bears," you're probably right! Some people are afraid they'll be eaten alive by them, others are worried that bruins will devour their food. The truth is, most bears are afraid of people and so keep pretty well hidden, at least during the day. It's at night, when you're asleep, that they become bold enough to raid your camp.

In my experience, the outfitter and government recommended rigamarole of caching food packs in trees, or on a pole or line strung between trees, is a waste of time and energy. Bears—and other bothersome beasts—won't get your food if you follow these simple rules:

1. Keep a clean camp. Pack out or burn all leftover food. If this is impractical, bury food wastes at least 150 feet from camp and water. And never throw left-over food down Forest Service box latrines. As mentioned in chapter 5, bears will knock over toilet boxes and climb into the pits to get edibles. The result is an indescribable mess!

2. Don't leave food in your tent! Even toothpaste and gum may attract hungry animals. Bears will tear your tent apart to get food!

3. Some canoeists place food packs under an overturned canoe and set cooking pots on the craft to function as a "night alarm" system. The idea is that if a bear comes along, it will be scared off by the sound of falling metal. Don't you believe it! Camp bears are not afraid of loud noises. If a bear can't figure out how to get food from under your canoe, it may pounce on or bite at the craft. A powerful black bear can probably chew through a Royalex™ or fiberglass canoe!

4. Animals learn from past experience where campers put their food. Once they discover some scraps, they'll be back for more. Ever notice how birds, mice and squirrels hang around the picnic table when people are present? Moving the table a few yards won't help, but eating in a place that is unfamiliar to animals will!

Fortunately, you can outsmart bothersome beasts by simply putting *odor-free* food in an unsuspecting place. For example, bears know from past experience that many campers put their food in trees. *Certain trees!* On popular campsites there is often only one tree with limbs high enough to discourage a determined bruin, and every canoe party hangs their food packs from it.

"Soon as it gets dark, I'll climb up there and get those packs," thinks the bear. And later, she—or one of her cubs—usually does. Black bears are good climbers; they are very skilled at getting food packs out of trees! Some clever bears even learn that if they rake the trunks of certain trees with their claws, a food pack may come crashing down. Of course, they probably have no idea that they simply severed the pulley rope you tied to the tree!

To outfox an experienced camp bear, simply break familiar memory patterns: *Don't put your food in the same place as everyone else!*

One solution is to take food packs out of the camp area, *well away from hiking trails, game paths and human traffic.* Be sure to seal your food in plastic, so there are no odors. The Forest Service wants you to hang your food packs *at least twelve feet off the ground, five feet below a branch, and ten feet from the nearest tree trunk.* Finding a tree that meets these specifications is like searching for the ideal campsite—a breezy, sun-exposed level spot with good drainage, convenient access to water, and enough tree cover to discourage high winds.

A perfect "bear tree" is as elusive as the perfect campsite! Simply lofting your pack into a convenient limb or, up to a pole or tight rope strung between two trees, will not deter a determined bear if everyone else uses the same system! On the other hand, grounding food packs where bears don't expect to find them, works like magic.

Here are some facts that support this observation:

Each year, from 1973 to 1987, friend Al Todnem and I each took two, seven day canoe trips with teenagers into the Boundary Waters. That's four weeks per summer, times fourteen years, or *fifty-six weeks* for the two of us. To this, add eighty days (eleven weeks) of solo canoe trips I've made with friends. The total is 56 + 11 = 67 weeks, or 1.3 years of continuous use.

Bear problems? Absolutely none. Zero. Nicht!

My method -*breaking the classical conditioning habit by grounding food packs in an unsuspecting area* discourages bears, mice, raccoons, birds and other critters. Indeed, I can happily report that in forty-one years of canoeing, I have never lost *anything* to wild animals. And this includes close encounters with two BWCA black bears, one Saskatchewan black bear, four tundra grizzlies in the Northwest Territories, seven Hudson Bay area polar bears, and a small pack of wolves near James Bay, Ontario.

These are the bear facts! Nonetheless, if you're still intent on treeing your food packs, just remember *not to use the same tree as everyone else!* Frankly, I'll stand by my statistics and suggest that lofting food into a tree each night is a good way to consume precious time that you could use swimming, drinking rich Columbian coffee or staring deep into a flickering fire.

Certainly, no method of caching food is foolproof, or proof against fools. And fools will set their food packs within yards of mainstream animal trails, thinking they've put them in the boonies.

Yes, bears are dumber than us—well, maybe dumber than most of us. Every system requires common sense, and some campers have none. In summary:

Animals are creatures of habit—they return to where they are regularly fed. If you put food where they expect it, don't be surprised if they get it! Every bird lover knows how difficult it is to outfox squirrels. Some of these little beggars get your bird seed no matter what you do. Sure, there are squirrel proof rigs, but they are clever, expensive, or time consuming to make or operate. And there are bear-proof trees too. The question is, do you want to go to the trouble of finding one—or of rigging a Rube Goldberg system of high ropes and pulleys—or, would you rather adopt a simple system that depends on skills, not things?

My friend, Tom Anderson, Director of Rose and Lee Warner Nature Center, in Marine, Minnesota, has written a wonderful book entitled, *Black Bears, Season's in the Wild*, which I commend to your attention. I've camped with Tom on numerous occasions, most recently on a canoe trip through polar bear country near Hudson's Bay. Tom never once suggested that we tree our packs, though he recommends it in his book. When I asked him why, he quietly told me it was "expected," then made me promise to never tell a soul. Sorry, Tom, too bad I didn't sign a blood oath!

HOW TO TELL IF A BEAR MIGHT VISIT YOUR CAMPSITE

It's a good idea to check out a prospective campsite before you commit to it for the night. Look for paper, plastic, foil and/or food remains in and around the fire grate, picnic table and box latrine. Be sure to scrutinize the toilet pit for food wastes. There should be none! Check the shallow water along shore for fish viscera and food. If you see significant foreign matter, move on to cleaner grounds. On the other hand, if everything is in good order, and you follow suit with a clean, odorless camp, it's almost certain you *won't* see a bear!

WHAT TO DO IF A BEAR COMES INTO CAMP!

Odds are the bear will come while you're asleep, possibly with a cub or two in tow. If you sense the presence of a bear, stay calm. It's your food he/she wants, not you! My somewhat casual procedure goes something like this:

I throw on some clothes, grab a flashlight and noisily emerge from my tent, curious to see the show. My dried food is vacuum-sealed in plastic and secured in plastic-lined Duluth packs which are scattered on the ground, outside my campsite. There are no food odors or visible food containers (packs!) to attract a hungry bruin, so there's little cause for concern. Invariably, the intruder will search the usual places—the "bear pole" or "tree," picnic table, fire place and box latrine—then, finding nothing, leave with a discouraging grunt. This scenario almost always plays true. On very rare occasions, the bear gets mad, tears at tents, canoes...and people! So I keep my distance. I make the bear aware of my presence but I do not intimidate it by throwing rocks or shining a light into its eyes. I just watch and wait. In ten minutes or so, the show will be over, the bear will leave, and I will return to bed.

Predacious attacks: Maybe one bear in 10,000 actively seeks human flesh. It happened in the Boundary Waters in 1987 and in Algonquin Provincial Park in 1992. The BWCA attack was unusual because a father and son watched the bear (a small female) peer at them from the edge of the forest for several minutes before she attacked. Convinced that the bear was merely curious, the man sent his son to gather firewood. As soon as the boy was out-of-sight, the bear galloped in. The man leapt into the lake and the bear followed suit. Ultimately, the son beat the bear with a canoe paddle and got his dad into a canoe, which saved his life. When Forest Service personnel later killed the bear, they discovered she was starving.

A more serious predacious episode occurred in Algonquin Provincial Park in 1992. A young man and woman were killed and eaten by a black bear while they were setting up camp. The couple were experienced and they had a clean camp. The bear was a healthy, average sized animal. Why the unprovoked attack? We can only surmise that there are crazy bears like there are crazy people. Fortunately, there aren't very many of them.

These grizzly cases make news because they are so rare. You are more likely to drown, be struck by lightning, killed by a falling tree, or shot by an enraged criminal than attacked by a black bear. Indeed, the chances of bear attack are so small they hardly deserve the ink in this chapter. Nonetheless, if you are attacked by a black bear, the rule is to *fight with all your might! Do not* lay down and play dead! More than likely you will survive the mauling.

Black bears often "mock" charge: They woof loudly and menacingly clack their teeth as they gallop towards you. The formula solution is to stand your ground, spread your arms wide and confidently call, "Whoa, bear!" Above all, *don't run!* Doing so, is almost certain to provoke an attack.

Here are some ways to further reduce being injured by a bear:

1. Bears don't like large numbers of people. Two people are much more likely to be attacked than six.

2. Evidence suggests you are safer to sleep in a tent than in the open. This is particularly true in grizzly country. Evidently, the big bears mistake a human in a sleeping bag for their natural food.

3. Oleo capsician, the flaming ingredient in red pepper, is a proven bear repellent. It comes in aerosol cans and has an effective range of up to 30 feet. Some formulations are more potent (and expensive!) than others, so check around before you buy. Be sure you get a holster so you can get at the product quickly.

ORNERY STINGERS

At the outset, I should make it perfectly clear that the T-shirt which bears a chest-filling likeness of a female mosquito and the legend, *Minnesota State Bird*, is no joke. At best, it is an "average sized" insect! The usual precautions— cover bare skin, slather on gobs of repellent, don't go out alone after dark and stay clear of swampy areas—do reduce encounters with these giant beasts. But the truth is, canoes and insects go hand-in-hand. It's a cruelty nature bestows upon Boundary Waters paddlers in return for the good times she provides.

Fortunately, bugs nearly always disappear when the sun comes out and the wind blows up. Build a smoldering fire and the usually determined critters chicken out and zoom to parts unknown. Retire to your screened-in tent and you can rest in peace until nature calls.

Frankly, an oblivious attitude is your best defense. Think "bugs don't bother me, bugs don't bother me!" and you won't notice if they do. But mix bad psychology with an ornery disposition, and the pesky critters will devour your hide!

Beyond mentality, there is science, and the usual array of protective measures. Topping the list is a *compact* head net. Bulky, military styles with draw cord hems which button down to breast pockets are a nuisance in the Boundary Waters where head nets go on and off with each passing wave of fighter planes. A simple rectangular net which, in a flash, can be wadded to fist size and stuffed into a hat crown or shirt pocket, is best.

Tightly woven cotton-polyester and/or nylon clothing will keep most bugs at bay. Clothes don't get much more bug-proof than inexpensive GI fatigues and chinos. Some bite-sensitive paddlers subscribe to over-kill and seal pant hems and shirt sleeves with Velcro™ strips. But few days are buggy enough to warrant this practice.

Surprisingly, the *color* of your clothes is important. Generally, dark hues attract insects. Tans, grays, greens and powder blues neither attract nor repel, but darker shades of blue, black or deep red, drive bugs wild. Navy blue—the most popular of all outdoor colors—is *absolutely the worst* color of all!

After clothes, comes repellents. Those high in the active ingredient DEET (n,n diethyl-m-toluamide) work best, though there are some health concerns. DEET is caustic to sensitive skin and high concentrations of the chemical produce allergic reactions in some people. Children and sensitive adults should choose herbal (Citronella) based formulas.

In my travels to the Northwest Territories of Canada, I've field tested just about every insect repellent known to man. Here's a summary of my findings, which I gathered from bites on my very own body!

1. Pure, or nearly pure DEET repels bugs best, but it is so caustic to skin, plastic pocket knife handles, glass frames, synthetic long underwear and plastic canoe parts, that I refuse to use it. Mild, cream-based repellents with 25-50 percent DEET, work nearly as well as full strength and they last much longer. They are also much less expensive than high-DEET products.

2. I dislike the oily feel of repellents, so I usually just daub the chemicals on my clothing—shirt cuffs, pant leg hems, inside hat brim, and a large red handkerchief which I wear around my neck. This keeps most insects away from my face, wrists and ankles.

3. Aerosol spray cans, though technically legal in the Boundary Waters, are not worth bringing along. Read the label and you'll see how ineffective and pricey they are. And, there's a bulky can to pack out!

BLACK FLIES AND NO-SEE-UMS

Black flies are more at home on fast moving rivers than lakes, so they seldom occur in epidemic proportions in the Boundary Waters. However, when these pesky gnats do appear, head nets or "bug jackets" (the kind anglers wear) are your only salvation. Repellents, by and large, merely discourage black flies. I've seen these ugly little insects swim in 50 percent DEET, then get up and fly away!

Black flies have an unusual habit of flying or climbing to the highest place. They'll swarm around your head, more so than your lower body. Raise up your hat on a canoe paddle and they'll follow suit. If you're very clever, you may be able to use this tactic to shag them on to a nearby friend!

If black flies get into your tent, don't panic. After a few minutes, they'll settle on the bug screen and begin to climb skywards. Let them have their little walk. When they reach the top of the net, slowly unzip the screen and heartlessly toss them back into the cruel world.

WHEN REPELLENTS FAIL, RETIRE TO YOUR "SUSIE BUG NET!"

First, you apply repellents to exposed skin. As more insects home in, you add a head net, then a DEET-impregnated bug jacket. Ultimately, you rant and swear, and in disgust, retire to your no-seeum-proof tent. Meanwhile, friends nearby enjoy a bug-free after dinner brandy and a glorious sunset inside their "Susie bug net" (figure 11-1)—personal bug armor designed by my wife, Sue Harings:

Materials needed: A piece of mosquito netting 60-72 inches wide and eight feet long, plus enough one-eighth inch diameter shock-cord to span the hem. Don't use no-seeum net; it's not strong enough and you can't see through it.

Procedure: Fold the netting lengthwise to produce a rectangular sheet which measures about eight feet by six feet. Sew up the two long sides, hem the bottom and install the bungee cord in the hem. The finished net will weigh less than a pound and compress to football size.

Figure 11-1

SUSIE BUG NET

Here are some uses for your Susie bug net:

1. Eat inside it; there's room for two adults or a pack of kids.
2. Sleep out under the stars. The net covers you from head to toe. Cinch the bungee cord tightly around the foot of your sleeping bag.
3. Use it as a "porta potty" when bugs are bad. It fully encompasses the official Forest Service "throne."
4. Swim in it! Amble to the beach as a ghostly apparition in your Susie bug net. Wear your life vest and you'll float confidently inside your bug armor. When you've had your swim, step assertively ashore and drape the netting over a rock to dry.
5. Gently lay the net over breads, cheese and lunch meats to keep flies away.
6. Rig a tripod inside and you have a tiny bug-proof tipi in which to wash dishes, cook and make repairs.

Protective netting is essential if there are children or bug-sensitive adults in your party. With a little practice you can hike, run and even paddle a canoe while wearing a Susie bug net! Roll and stuff your Susie bug net under a pack flap so it will be available at meals and rest stops.

NO-SEE-UMS

No-see-ums are similar to black-flies, but they are much smaller and less menacing. Whereas black fly bites may bleed and swell for days, no-see-um bites sting for a few seconds then produce short-lived red welts. But, no-see-ums attack by the thousands and they're so small they fly right through standard mesh tent screens, head nets, and...Susie bug nets!

The solution is to cover up completely *and* apply repellents on exposed skin and wide-meshed mosquito screens. Most modern tents have fine-mesh netting which discourages no-see-ums and the free passage of air. Unfortunately, no-see-ums usually appear on hot, muggy days when you'd give anything for a welcome breeze. So in the end, it's a toss-up: If your tent is equipped with fine mesh netting, you get no no-see-ums and no ventilation. If it has standard mosquito netting, you enjoy a cool night of swatting bugs!

Frankly, no-see-ums are relatively rare in the Boundary Waters. When they do appear, you can usually discourage them by treating standard mesh mosquito screens with repellents. Or, simply close the nylon door panel which, of course, stifles the air.

CHAPTER TWELVE

Dangers, Safety & First-Aid

Newcomers to the Boundary Waters commonly express three fears: *Bugs, bears, and bad weather.* "Bugs and bears," as we've learned from the last chapter, are largely a perceived threat. The *real* dangers are lightning storms and whitecaps, capsizing far from shore in frigid water, high winds, falling trees (widow-makers), hypothermia-producing cold, wrecking your canoe in a rapid, and becoming injured while portaging or swimming. There are also burns, cuts, water-borne parasites, eye injuries and, God forbid, a gasoline stove that explodes in your face (it happened to me!). Any one of these events may end your canoe trip on the spot and leave you wondering how you'll get back to your car. Here's how to avoid these common dangers, and to treat their effects when you can't!

SWIMMING DON'TS!

1. *Absolutely no diving—ever!* I once reprimanded some teenagers for diving off a high cliff on Gunflint Lake. Their leader curtly advised me to "stay out of our business," so I shut my mouth and paddled on to my campsite which was about half a mile away. Later, that evening, two canoes-full of kids from the group I earlier admonished, stopped at my camp and tearfully asked directions to the public landing. They told me that shortly after I left, one of the boys dove head-first into a submerged rock. The adult leader flagged down the driver of a passing fishing boat who took him and the boy to the road head and on to the hospital in Grand Marais. The leader told the kids to paddle out and wait for him at nearby Gunflint Lodge.

After our trip we were horrified to learn that the boy died from the concussion. This solitary event suggests that diving of any kind is unsafe on a canoe trip!

2. ***Don't swim barefooted!*** On the first day of my first school-sponsored canoe trip, a fourteen year old girl badly cut her big toe while swimming barefoot in a rocky area. Since then, I have required that shoes be worn while swimming. I suggest you adopt a similar policy.

3. ***Don't swim alone!*** This rule is cardinal in every tripping camp in the country, and for good reason. If suddenly you cramp while swimming, or a breeze blows you far from shore, you'll wish you had a friend to tow you in or yell a warning. If you want to cover all bases, wear your life jacket when you swim.

4. ***Don't go into the water until you have identified a safe escape route to shore.*** I've watched tired swimmers struggle to obtain a secure foothold on sharp or slippery rocks—another reason to wear shoes when you swim! I sometimes tie a long "exit rope" to a heavy rock or tree to help swimmers climb ashore.

LIGHTNING (figure 12-1)

A canoe (any canoe!) on open water is a perfect lightning rod, so get ashore at the first hint of thunder. Nonetheless, converting advice to practice isn't easy if there are big waves and a rocky shoreline. Often, you may have no choice but to paddle on to a campsite, portage or protected cove.

A "cone of protection" extends from the tops of the tallest trees or hills outward about 45 degrees in all directions. Paddle within this protected zone, but not so close to its center that lightning may jump to you. Lightning can jump 30 feet or more, so 50-100 feet from shore may be the best place to be. When you find a place to land, seek a low-lying spot away from the tall trees near the water's edge. A rocky over-hang provides good protection and makes a fine umbrella under which to wait out the rain.

IF YOU AWAKEN TO A LIGHTNING STORM

Scenario: You're awakened from a sound sleep by the loud crack of thunder. Rain is coming down in sheets and white lightning dances across the sky. What to do?

The textbook solution is to leave your tent and wait out the storm in a low, protected area. But your tightly pitched tent is dry inside and standing firm in the persistent wind. Wearily, you unzip a window and peer at the worsening storm.

Figure 12-1

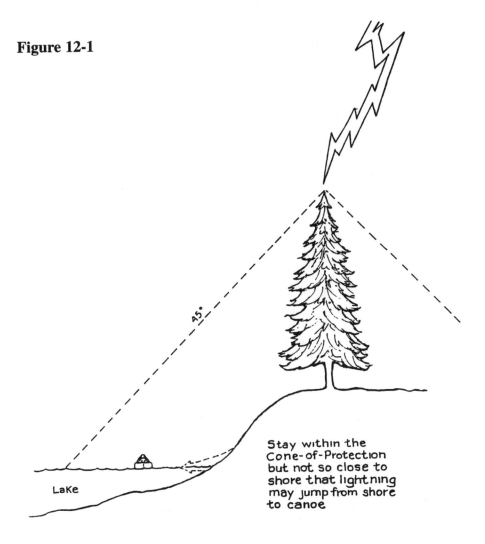

45°

Lake

Stay within the
Cone-of-Protection
but not so close to
shore that lightning
may jump from shore
to canoe

"S'pose we should get outa here before we get fried?" you remark to your friend, who has just begun to stir.

"You gotta be kidding," comes the sleepy answer. "Leave this tent? Never! See ya in the morning, buddy."

If you plan to stay put, take these precautions: Sit up on your *dry* foam sleeping pad. Draw up your knees so that only your buttocks and soles of your feet touch the insulated pad. Thus, if you do get burned from a nearby strike, the electricity will (hopefully) miss your heart.

Be aware that all is lost if your bedding gets wet—a condition you can prevent by always using a plastic groundcloth *inside* your tent!

FIRST-AID FOR LIGHTNING BURNS

Lightning hits a tree thirty feet from a tent located at the opposite end of your campsite. You dress hastily and run to your friends, one of whom is unresponsive and not breathing. One of his shoes is missing and there is a small, deep burn on the sole of his foot.

Diagnosis? Electrocution—an apparent cardiac arrest!

Treatment: High-voltage electricity usually kills people by producing cardiac arrest. It may also paralyze the respiratory system. If the person is alive, the burns are probably minor and can be attended to later. Your immediate concern is to get the person's heart and respiratory system functioning.

Begin CPR immediately! If you can restore heart rhythm and breathing, you can probably save your friend.

This accomplished, keep the patient warm and send for help immediately. Electrocution may cause disorientation, coma, seizures and spinal cord injuries. It may also rupture the ear drums. All you can do till help arrives is to keep your friend immobilized and warm, and convince him that he'll be okay.

WIDOW-MAKERS

"Widow-maker" is forestry slang for a wind-downed tree that gets caught in the branches of another tree as it falls to the ground. The first good breeze drops some widow-makers, others remain hung up for decades. Occasionally, you'll find these dangerous snags poised menacingly over beautiful tent sites. I caution you to resist the urge to cut down or remove branches from these trees, or to pitch your camp in the probable path of their fall. Widow-makers are under tremendous tension. If one splits under the pressure of a saw, or comes crashing down on you at night, you may awaken in another world! Snag removal is a job for Forest Service professionals!

WHEN YOUR CANOE BECOMES A KITE!

I was napping on Miles Island on Saganaga Lake on a testy June day when a sudden squall came up. I always make it a practice to tie my overturned, beached canoe to a tree before I wander off or retire to my tent. However, this time I did not follow my own advice.

Suddenly, the wind lashed out with uncommon fury and turned my eighteen foot lightweight aluminum canoe into a kite! The craft sailed overhead, end-for-end (!) then dropped into the waves about 100 feet from shore. Barefoot and clad in a swim suit, I quickly zipped on my life vest and dove in after it. Thank goodness there was a long tracking line with which to tow the canoe ashore. I suffered a bruised foot and badly injured pride. I also learned to practice what I preach!

Inverting and tying unattended canoes to a tree or boulder is an expedition axiom that every canoeist should embrace. Every season in the Boundary Waters, canoes blow out to sea. And, red-faced canoeists swim after them!

On a similar note, never store your paddles in the open or on sloping rock where wind or rain could carry them into the lake. Leaned against a tree, under an overturned canoe near water, or along a walking path, *is not* a safe place. I lay my paddles on the ground, alongside my tent. I am careful to turn bent-shaft paddle blades *up,* so they won't break if I accidentally step on them.

SAFETY WITH EDGED TOOLS

Cuts from whittling are the most common injury among teenagers. The rule of thumb is to bring *three* bandaids per kid. Or, carry fewer bandages and outlaw whittling!

Tips: You won't lose your pocket knife if you tie it to a nylon lanyard which is attached to your belt. Or, place the knife in your pocket and stuff a large handkerchief on top.

Axe: If you use your hand axe as a simple splitting wedge, as suggested in chapter 10, you'll eliminate most accidents. *Keep your axe sheathed, and in a pack* when it's not being used. *Never* leave an axe stuck in a log—someone could trip over it! If you must set down an unsheathed axe for a short time, place the axe on its side, blade tucked under a heavy log or rock, as illustrated in figure 12-3.

Figure 12-3

For Safety Sake

A safe place for your folding saw: Most canoeists leave their folding saw by the wood pile, figuring it will come in handy later—a practice that can be dangerous, especially if there are exposed teeth and failing light. A colleague learned this lesson on a canoe trip with teenagers. Two kids were horsing around, when one lost his balance and fell, lightly brushing the saw, which was leaning teeth out, against a tree. Fortunately, the youngster only suffered a minor cut. Figure 12-4 suggests two reasonably safe ways to store a saw when it is not *folded and packed!*

Figure 12-4

WATER QUALITY

More than 200,000 people a year use the Boundary Waters—reason enough to boil, filter or chemically treat every drop of water you drink. Water tests conducted in the early 1980's by my own ninth grade environmental science students, suggest that water taken from shallow lakes, beaver streams, and near popular campsites, is not safe to drink. Play the odds long enough, and you'll probably get burned!

Nonetheless, a lot (probably the majority) of canoeists draw water where they find it and don't give quality a second thought. A minority (myself included) boil or filter questionable water and/or follow these rules religiously:

1. Never take water from shallows or within 100 feet of a campsite. Sometimes, I weight my water pail with a rock and submerge the pail thirty feet or more on a long rope.
2. Don't drink "green" water. It contains algae which harbor microorganisms. Water colored brown from natural tree-produced tannins, is fine.
3. Friendly microorganisms need oxygen to decompose wastes in water. For this reason, water taken from wavy or turbulent places is more likely to be safe than that drawn from stagnant areas or wind protected bays.
4. Don't take water from beaver streams! Beaver are the favored host of Giardia lambia—a protozoan that can make you plenty sick.
5. Ultraviolet light kills microorganisms. Take your drinking water from a sunny place!

WATER TREATMENT PROCEDURES

Boiling: Bring the water to a minimal boil and you'll kill everything except the most resistant spores which are almost never present in the wilderness—and which can only be destroyed by pressurized heat above the boiling point. If you need more heat than 212 degrees Fahrenheit, you need a pressure cooker!

Chemicals: All chemicals make water taste bad, reason enough to avoid them. Boiling, and germicidal filters are faster and more reliable, and they preserve the good fresh taste you drove hundreds of miles to experience!

Filters: Most filtration units are cumbersome, delicate, slow to use and hard to clean. There are exceptions, notably the high speed PUR "Explorer," which filters one liter of water per minute and cleans in seconds with a twist of the pump handle. The PUR "Scout," a smaller, less expensive version of the "Explorer," is another excellent choice.

PUR filters received worldwide attention in 1989 when two shipwrecked sailors relied on its manually operated desalination pump to survive 66 days in a life raft adrift in the Pacific Ocean. The PUR combines microfiltration with an antimicrobial tri-iodine resin system that kills bacteria and infectious viruses. A replaceable carbon filter absorbs the objectionable iodine aftertaste.

MEDICINE FOR THE BOUNDARY WATERS

Wilderness first-aid classes tend to emphasize bone-crushing falls and internal injuries which are more often associated with hiking and mountaineering accidents than the common ailments you are likely to experience in the Boundary Waters.

For example, in 20 years of guiding canoe trips, no one in my charge has ever suffered a broken limb, head injury or pulmonary disorder. But I have treated scores of blisters, sprains, scratched corneas, ear infections (swimmer's ear), insect bites, burns, embedded fishhooks, and illness due to water-born parasites. These are the medical problems that everyone who treks to the Boundary Waters should be prepared to treat.

In preparing this section, I kept uppermost in mind that:
- Most outdoors people have little in-depth first-aid knowledge and no inclination to learn. It follows that wilderness first aid procedures should be easy to master, quick to administer, and correct!
- Sanitary conditions are difficult to attain in the woods. Nonetheless, many first-aid techniques require sterile techniques. Canoeists need to know simple ways to clean wounds.
- The wilderness "first-aider" must adopt treatment procedures which reflect realistic field conditions. For example, you may not be able to leave a (taped down) fish hook embedded in the skin or keep a victim off a bad sprain if he or she must help paddle and portage the canoe and do camp chores.
- Most canoeists don't want to carry a sophisticated first-aid kit. If it won't fit in a one pound coffee can, it will probably be left at home!

Not everyone has the time or discipline to master the advanced medical techniques needed to treat heavy-duty fractures, gashes, and head wounds. However, everyone can, in a few hours, learn how to treat the common ailments which are most likely to be encountered on a canoe trip.

With these thoughts, I offer the following field-proven, physician-recommended techniques for treating the most common back-country injuries, along with suggestions for building a small but useful first aid kit. Space does not permit detailing all you need to know about the described conditions. If you're serious about wilderness medicine, you'll seek authoritative knowledge through books[1].

FIRST AID KIT: SUGGESTED CONTENTS

An antiseptic, pain-reliever, anti-inflammatory drug and antibiotic ointment, plus an over-the-counter remedy for burns and insect bites, are the major medications you'll need. To this, add an antacid, tape, gauze, compresses and bandaids, and you're set for most emergencies.

THE MINI-FIRST-AID KIT

Here's the bare minimum if you want to go light:
- 4 eye patches
- Spenco 2nd Skin
- Microfoam tape
- Triple antibiotic ointment
- Four bandaids
- Small roll of bandage gauze
- Aspirin, Tylenol™ or Ibuprofin™
- Small tube of Polysporin™ ophthalmic ointment (Rx), or Yellow oxide of mercury, ophthalmic 2%, (non-Rx).
- Antacid tablets

[1]WILDERNESS MEDICINE Beyond First Aid, *4th Edition* by William W. Forgey, M.D. (ICS Books), Suggests sensible first aid kits and medical advice, for persons going into the Boundary Waters, for only $14.99.

THE MOST COMMON AILMENTS

Fish-Hook in the Skin

The common advice is to work the embedded barb through the skin, cut off the barb and extract the hook. But this won't work if the hook is embedded to the curve. In any case, extraction will be painful unless you inject the entrance hole of the fish-hook with 1-2 ml of *Xylocaine*. Wait a few minutes for the drug to take effect, then complete the extraction. Don't be scared off by the *Xylocaine* injection: There's no way you can mess up.

A virtually painless method of extraction without Xylocaine, is illustrated in figure 12-5.

Figure 12-5

Procedure:

1. Loop light cord or fish line around the curve of the hook.
2. Push the eye of the hook firmly against the surface of the skin.
3. While holding the shank down, firmly jerk the cord.

This method works so well that the victim often doesn't know when the hook is out!

Note: The "string-pull" technique works best in areas like the shoulder, back of head, and parts of the torso and extremities that have little connective tissue. *Don't* use this procedure if the hook is lodged in the fingers or near an eye, in which case, surgical extraction with *Xylocaine* is recommended. If you are unsure of your extraction skills, tape the fishhook in place, so it won't do further damage, and evacuate the victim to a hospital.

FOREIGN BODY IN THE EYE

First, try to flush out the foreign body with *Eye Stream*™. If that fails, have the patient look straight ahead while you shine a light into the eye from one side. If you see a speck (lift the upper eye lid and check here, too), gently brush it away with a cotton Q-tip. If there is any pain or redness, lace the lower lid with *Neosporin ophthalmic ointment (Rx)*, or *Yellow oxide of mercury, ophthalmic 2% (non-Rx)*. The patient should close his/her eyes until the medication melts. If pain persists, bandage *both* eyes shut with eye patches and micro-foam tape.

DISLOCATED SHOULDER

A dislocated shoulder is one of the most common and painful ailments in canoeing. Relocation is easy if you use the *Stimson* method illustrated in figure 12-6.

Procedure:

1. Place the victim face down on a flat, elevated platform. An over-turned canoe will do. Tie an approximate 10 pound weight to the wrist of the fully extended arm with a soft neckerchief or padded belt. As the muscles tire, the victim will relax and the shoulder will relocate. What could be simpler? Or safer?

Figure 12-6

STIMSON METHOD
TO RE-LOCATE A
DISLOCATED SHOULDER

FRICTION BLISTER ON THE HEEL

If a friction blister develops, it will have to be lanced. First, wash it with soap and open it along one edge with a sharp pen-knife. Use your butane lighter to sterilize the knife. Express the fluid then apply *Triple Antibiotic Ointment*. Top this with a piece of *Spenco 2nd Skin*, held in place with the *Spenco* knit bandage.

Alternative method: Clean and lance the blister as above. Apply antibiotic ointment and cover with *two* eye patches and *microfoam tape*. The combination patches/tape provide substantial cushioning for the blister site.

Space prohibits detailing all the things you need to know to treat these and other conditions. But I won't omit the best advice of all, which is to *slow down and think before you act*. Avoid the accident and you won't need all that good first-aid gear you brought along!

SIGNALS: WHEN YOU NEED TO BRING THE AIRPLANE DOWN!

It was 1967, and my first trip to the Boundary Waters. My friend John Orr and I had just completed the portage into knife lake when we came upon a group of teenagers. Amidst the canoes and equipment was a stretcher, occupied by a 15-year old girl.

The girl told us she had a severe stomach ache and would be okay in a few days. John, an old football coach, questioned her further, then gently touched a side of her abdomen. Immediately, she wreaked with pain. John's diagnosis was "appendicitis!"

We suggested that the leaders immediately paddle the girl to Cache Bay Ranger station, where there was a radio telephone. But, before they could comply, we spotted a Forest Service fire plane overhead. I whipped out my mirror-equipped Silva Ranger compass and flashed the pilot's eye. The plane landed and ferried the youngster to the hospital in Grand Marais. When John and I returned from our trip we learned that the girl's appendix had been removed without complication, and with just hours to spare!

A mirror is well worth bringing along on a Boundary Waters trip. An official military heliograph (the kind with the hole in the center) is much easier to use than a standard mirror. Ultra light signaling mirrors are available at most camping shops.

Smoke: There are a lot of smoky campfires in the BWCA, so it's doubtful you can bring down a plane or attract a Forest Service canoe with one. However, "colored smoke" is almost certain to attract help. Orange smoke grenades with 50 second burning times are available at every marina and sailing shop. You may want to consider carrying some if you will be more than two days paddle from help.

CHAPTER THIRTEEN

A Magic Day in the BWCA

Sunrise on a quiet lake deep in the heart of the Boundary Waters Canoe Area. Anxious hands, chilled by the day's beginning, slip the trim Kevlar canoe into the champagne-clear water. Only the muffled chirp of a Canada Jay testifies to the day's awakening.

You muscle your gear to the water's edge and, with the help of your partner, methodically place it into the canoe. The natural odor of sweat-stained canvas and hand-oiled leather suggest that these old Duluth packs "belong."

It takes less than a minute to orient your map and set a compass bearing to the first portage which, by your calculation is more than two miles away. Briefly, you glance at your watch—it's a quarter past seven. An hour of casual paddling will bring you to the first carry of the day.

You're paddling stern today, so you have the luxury of a "shock-corded" thwart that keeps your oriented map from blowing out to sea. Strapped around the thwart is a handy wrist compass which you can read without putting down your paddle.

For awhile, you paddle determinedly along, eyes intent on a distant notch on the horizon, beyond which is the portage. Then, suddenly aware that you are hurrying for no reason, you call a pause and laze back in the canoe and drop your arms to your sides, hands immersed wrist-deep in the cool clear water. Every muscle relaxes as your body attunes to the growing warmth of the expanding sun. Overhead, a lone cottony cloud punctuates an ocean of azure. Here, there are no schedules or deadlines to meet, no intellectual discussions or arguments. There is just the magic of the water.

Ultimately, you are awakened by the hushed enthusiasm of your partner. "There, there!" she whispers, pointing to a full grown moose, one-hundred feet away. "Freeze; just float," you quietly command. Startled, but unafraid, the huge animal stares curiously your way. Then, with an unhurried air, she swims lazily ashore and disappears into the forest.

It is barely eight a.m. and already the wind is producing small whitecaps on the formerly placid water. Thank goodness you are now in the lee of the islands. Momentarily, you rest your paddle on the gunnels and study the map. "The portage is in that bay to the right," you call confidently. "No, I think it's over there," answers your partner, who motions toward a narrow stream at left.

Her destination is closer, so you go there first. Sure enough, she is right on target—a small opening near the channel marks the carry.

You put ashore at the 80 rod portage but don't unload the canoe. The rough looking trail suggests that either few people come this way or there's a "paddle through" to the next lake. "Let's check out the beaver stream before we carry over," you call enthusiastically.

The stream is clear for the first hundred yards. Then, it disappears in a maze of thick vegetation.

"Think we can get through?" asks your friend.

"Don't know. Wanna try?"

"Sure," comes the ready reply.

At the start, the beaver stream is narrow and deep, with plenty of water to float a canoe. Round the bend, it sprawls to a shallow pond and there's a low dam which you must carry over. Then, you're back in the skinny channel again and it's a smooth ride to the next lake.

Smugly, you congratulate one another on your adventurous spirits and the portage you didn't make!

It is noon and the high golden sun has flooded the day with warmth and light. High in the crown of a lofty white pine is a huge eagle nest which must weigh a quarter ton. In a flash, a mature bald eagle becomes airborne and silently glides your way. Disturbed by your presence, it emits a concerned "keeow!"

You put ashore on a lichen-splashed outcrop and prepare the lunch. Pita bread, laced with vacuum-sealed dill cheese, summer sausage and spicy brown mustard, go down easily with crystal lemonade you mix in a poly bottle. It has been an unusually interesting day so you agree to share one of the six crisp Braeburn apples you have brought along for special occasions.

The meal closes with a thorough policing of the lunch site. Every bit of garbage, from the tiniest twistie to the smallest rubber band is zealously rounded up and placed in a heavy duty plastic bag to be later burned at the campfire or *packed out* to civilization. To leave evidence—even the smallest evidence—of humankind on this treasured site is unthinkable. You don't need official rules and preaching to tell you what is right.

By three p.m. you have covered ten miles, which was your goal for the day. You've run two bouncy rapids, portaged five times and cheated a sixth carry by paddling a beaver stream to the next lake. High on a proud granite hill, a windward campsite commands a full view of the sparkling lake. "Let's camp there," you say unanimously. Then together you burst out laughing and agree that a long cool swim and coffee brewed fresh over a crackling fire would be a perfect way to end this perfect day. As you put ashore on the idyllic site you make a pact not to take the day's events too seriously. After all, tomorrow may be another magic day.

Equipment Check List

Many experienced Boundary Waters paddlers use an equipment checklist similar to the one below. They lay out on the floor all their equipment, then they check off items as they are packed. I almost always follow this procedure. On the few trips where I didn't, I have paid dearly. Once, I left behind my tool/repair kit; on another occasion I forgot my L.L. Bean boots and dish washing materials. Use this checklist as a guide, modify it to suit your needs, then follow it religiously! Space is provided for you to add your favorite items.

Tip: People who are new to the Boundary Waters usually bring *too much.* Some experienced outdoors people sort their gear into three piles—the *essentials,* the *almost essentials and luxuries.* They take all of the first pile, none of the second, and one luxury item!

CHECKLIST OF GEAR FOR A PARTY OF TWO PEOPLE FOR ONE WEEK

Group Equipment

❑ Four person tent (7'9' size), preferably with self-supporting framework.

❑ Plastic groundcloth for use inside the tent.

❑ 10' x 10' (or larger) coated nylon rain tarp, with a half dozen stakes and 100 feet of cord to rig it.

❑ 3 Duluth packs (#3 size), or 2 packs and a hard-shelled "wanigan" box or pack basket.

❑ Waterproof plastic liners for the Duluth packs.

❑ 50 feet of 1/4 inch diameter nylon rope.

❑ Folding saw.

- ❑ All steel hand axe.
- ❑ Repair and tool kit: "Leatherman," "Gerber multipliers" or similar multi-purpose tool, instant epoxy, repair kit for eyeglasses, needle and thread, buttons, copper rivets, duct tape, file, sharpening stone.
- ❑ Sponge for cleaning the canoe.
- ❑ Fillet knife or sheath knife.
- ❑ Pocket knife.
- ❑ Cook kit, teakettle or coffee pot, silverware.
- ❑ Dish washing materials: 3-M nylon scratcher, small bottle of biodegradable detergent, absorbent synthetic "pack towel" for dish drying.
- ❑ Graduated 2-quart plastic shaker, for bailing the canoe and mixing instant drink mixes.
- ❑ Stove and gasoline: Allow two liters of gasoline per week for a party of two.
- ❑ Cigarette lighter and matches in waterproof containers.
- ❑ Fire Ribbon™ or other emergency chemical fire-starting material.
- ❑ Small pocket thermometer to settle temperature arguments.
- ❑ One large candle to aid in starting fires.
- ❑ First-aid kit in waterproof container.

Individual Equipment

- ❑ Life jacket
- ❑ Two paddles: One lightweight for lakes, one heavyweight for rocky shallows.
- ❑ Sleeping bag and foam pad.
- ❑ 1 long-sleeved wool shirt.
- ❑ 2 cotton T-shirts.
- ❑ 1 tightly woven, insect-resistant, long-sleeved cotton-polyester shirt.
- ❑ 1 medium-weight wool, pile or acrylic sweater.
- ❑ 1 pair lightweight polyester, wool or polypropylene, two piece, long johns.
- ❑ 1 ultralight nylon windshell (not waterproof). Rolls to fist size.
- ❑ 4 pairs heavy wool socks.
- ❑ 4 pairs lightweight wool, polypropylene or polyester "liner" socks. *Tip:* Wear liner socks inside out so seams won't contact skin and cause blisters.
- ❑ 2 pairs long trousers—army fatigues are ideal. *Don't bring blue jeans!*
- ❑ Lightweight nylon bathing suit.

❑ Light nylon shorts for blistering hot days.

❑ Cotton web belt—dries faster than leather.

❑ 3 changes of underwear.

❑ Toiletries: Biodegradable soap, toothbrush, comb, small towel, etc.

❑ Chapstick and hand lotion (very important!).

❑ 2 large cotton bandannas: *Tip:* Saturate bandanna with bug dope and tie it around your neck to prevent insects from biting your face. Also useful for grabbing hot pots. You won't lose your pocket knife if you wad up your hanky and place it in your pants pocket over the knife.

❑ 1 pair of comfortable running shoes for camp use.

❑ 1 pair of sturdy 6-10 inch high boots (I prefer L.L. Bean's) for portaging.

❑ Light pair of gloves for cold days. Acrylic gloves with "rubber dots" are ideal.

❑ Small flashlight.

❑ Map set in waterproof case.

❑ Extra map.

❑ Insect repellent.

❑ Compact head net for use when insects are bad.

❑ Two-piece rain suit.

❑ 1 brimmed hat for sun (with chin strap); 1 wool stocking cap for chilly days. A fully waterproof hat is useful.

❑ Extra glasses if you wear them.

❑ Sunglasses.

❑ Security strap for glasses.

❑ Camera and film, plus waterproof camera bag.

❑ Compact binoculars for viewing wildlife.

❑ Compact fishing gear—3 Meps™ spinners, 3 Rapala's, 3 Daredevils,

❑ 2 jigs and a silver spoon, is enough. *Tip:* Store rods in protective plastic cases when paddling and portaging. Put your reel in an old sock and set it at the top of your pack, just under the closing flap.

❑ Journal, pencil, paperback book for rainy days.

❑ _____

❑ _____

❑ _____

❑ _____

Addresses

BWCA Reservation Service
P.O. Box 450
Cumberland, Maryland 21501
Phone 1-800-745-3399

(Write or call for Boundary Waters reservations. Permits cost $7.00 and may be charged to VISA/Mastercard/Discover)

Headquarters, Superior National Forest
P.O. Box 338
Duluth, MN 55801
Phone (218) 720-5324

(Request free pamphlet, *Welcome to the Superior National Forest*)

Quetico Provincial Park
District Manager, Ministry of Natural Resources
Atikokan, Ontario Canada POT 1CO
Phone (807) 597-2735

(Write or call for park permits, fishing licenses, and rules and regulations for canoeing in Quetico Provincial Park.)

Canadian Customs: (807) 274-3751
Canadian Immigration: (807) 274-3815
U.S. Customs: (218) 720-5201

Minnesota Dept. of Natural Resources
Box 40, 500 Lafayette Square
St. Paul, MN 55146
1-800-285-2000

Your source of hunting, fishing and trapping information. Fishing licenses are available by mail from the DNR.

Minnesota Dept. of Natural Resources
License Bureau; 500 Lafayette Square
St. Paul, MN 55146
1-800-285-2000

Watercraft in Minnesota *must* be licensed unless they are currently licensed in another state. Licenses cost $12.00 for three years, and are available by mail from the DNR office in Lafayette Square. Having an unlicensed canoe is a misdemeanor in Minnesota and is subject to a fine of $10 to $700.

Lake States Interpretive Association
HCR9, Box 600
International Falls, MN 56649
(218)-283-2103

Lake States Interpretive Association is a non-profit organization that supports the publication and sales of educational materials to visitors to the areas it serves. Request their free catalog of BWCA and Superior National Forest related maps, books and recreation guides.

EMERGENCY NUMBERS

Cook County Sheriff	*Lake County Sheriff*	*St. Louis County Sheriff*
Grand Marais, Minnesota	Ely: (218)-365-3344	Duluth: (218)-723-3754
(218)-387-1660	Two Harbors: (218)-834-2251	Ely: (218)-365-3344
		Virginia: (218)-741-1585

You can also forward messages to county sheriffs through the city police departments of Ely (218-365-3222) and Grand Marais (218-387-1120).

Friends of the Boundary Waters Wilderness
1313 Fifth St. S.E., Suite 329
Minneapolis, MN 55414
(612)-379-3835

"The Friends," as they are known, are the leading environmental watchdogs for the Boundary Waters Canoe Area and adjacent Quetico Provincial Park. They produce a quarterly newsletter, which keeps members abreast of ecological concerns. They also sponsor the production of BWCA specific environmental education materials for schools and nature centers. Membership is $25 per year. The organization's director Kevin Proescholdt is a serious environmental activist whose thought-provoking articles regularly appear in national magazines.

BWCA Wilderness Education Consortium
1313 5th St. S.E. #329
Minneapolis, MN 55414
(612) 379-3835

Source of two quality videos that describe low impact camping techniques for the Boundary Waters Canoe Area. Michael Tezla, an actor with the Guthrie Theater in Minneapolis portrays the experienced camper in the 21 minute version of *Leave No Trace—A Wilderness Ethic*. A shorter, six minute version of the video is also available. The videos are very inexpensive.

AREA RESORTS AND OUTFITTERS

Cook Chamber of Commerce
P.O. Box 59
Cook, MN 55723
1-800-648-5897

Crane Lake Commercial Club
Crane Lake, MN 55725
1-800-362-7405

Ely Chamber of Commerce
1660 E. Sheridan St.
Ely, MN 55731
(218)-365-6123

Lutsen-Tofte Tourism Association
Box 2248
Tofte, MN 55615
(218)-663-7804

Tip of the Arrowhead Association
Grand Marais, MN 55604
(218)-387-2524
1-800-622-4014

MAPS

McKenzie Map Company
315 West Michigan St., Suite 10
Duluth, MN 55802
(218)-727-2113

Drawn on a scale of 2" to the mile (1:31,680) , McKenzie maps are beautifully printed on nearly indestructible /waterproof POLYART 2 or TYVEK paper. McKenzie maps have crisp contour lines, specified contour intervals and accurate declination diagrams which show the difference between true and magnetic north.

W.A. Fisher Company
P.O. Box 1107
Virginia, MN 55792

W.A. Fisher Company maps are printed on waterproof paper and are reproduced in a variety of scales from 1/3" to the mile to 2-1/2" to the mile. Contour intervals and declination information are not specified. Large scale hydrographic maps of the most popular fishing lakes are available.

U.S. Geological Survey Map Sales

P.O. Box 25286, Federal Center, Bldg. 810

Denver, Colorado 80225

Your source of highly accurate topographic maps. Request a free *Index to Minnesota topographic maps*. Note: USGS maps do not indicate the location of portages, campsites and hiking trails.

Canada Map Office

615 Booth St.

Ottawa, Ontario Canada K1AOE9

Request free Index #1, which covers Ontario and Quetico Provincial Park. Also ask for the free pamphlet *Maps & Wilderness Canoeing*, which contains a wealth of useful information for canoeists.

Viking Safety Products

710 Raymond Ave.

St. Paul, MN 55114

1-800-328-6505 or (612)-646-6374

Source of sturdy, low cost industrial grade rain gear, plastic Duluth pack liners and rubber boots of all kinds.

Harvest Foodworks

66 Victoria Ave.

Smiths Falls, Ontario, Canada K7A 2P4

Tel 1-800-268-4268

Fax (613) 284-0284

Source of some of the tastiest trail foods around. Meatless dishes and the wonderful "Bill's Multigrain Cereal" recommended in chapter 9. Fast, easy preparation and ample portions for hungry voyageurs.

Foodsaver, by Tilia™

I vacuum seal many of my foods to prevent spoilage. I've had good luck with a powerful vacuum sealing machine called the FOODSAVER, which is available from Nationwide Marketing, Inc. 1550 Bryant St., Suite 850, San Francisco, CA 94103. Phone 1-800-777-5452. The product is also available from Cabela's, Inc. 812-13th Ave., Sidney, NB 69160. Phone 1-800-237-4444.

Caldwell Outdoor Enterprises
1335 West 11th
Port Angeles, WA 98362
(206)-457-3009

Mail order source of "bear mace"—a powerful cayenne pepper based spray that discourages determined bruins (and people!) without hurting them. Expensive, and worth it. Large and small versions are available. The large, one pound "Counter Assault" has an effective range of about ten meters, plus enough product to sustain several long bursts. Designed *for use on animals* (an illustrated bear is pictured on the label), it is one of the few "mace like" products which are legal in Canada. Order the handy holster or tape a snap clip to the can.

Indiana Camp Supply, Inc.
125 East 37th St.
PO Box 2166
Loveland, CO 80539
1-800-759-HIKE

Good source of outdoor gear, and about the only source of specialized first-aid items like the ones suggested in chapter 12. Very fast delivery.

Recovery Engineering, Inc.
Manufacturer of PUR water filtration devices
2229 Edgewood Ave. South
Minneapolis, MN 55426

I heartily recommend the PUR Explorer and Scout. Both units are fast and easy to use.

PACKSACKS, MAP CASES AND OTHER CANOEING LUGGAGE

Cooke Custom Sewing
7290 Stagecoach Trail
Lino Lakes, MN 55014-1988
(612) 784-8777

Cooke Custom Sewing was sold about five years ago. The new company went bankrupt and Dan Cooke is again manufacturing high grade outdoor gear under his own name. Cooke equipment is designed by serious outdoors people for use by serious outdoors people. Solid, reasonably priced stuff, no cutesy items. Dan Cooke manufactures the canoe splash covers which I designed, and which are described in my book, *Canoeing Wild Rivers.*

Grade VI Ltd.
P.O. Box 8
Urbana, IL 61801-0008
(217) 328-6666 or (612) 222-2917

Charlie Wilson's GRADE VI equippage is internationally known. Well designed, incredibly tough stuff, and the best map case around.

Granite Gear
Industrial Park, P.O. Box 278
Two Harbors, MN 55616
(218) 834-6157

Superior grade nylon canoe packs, thwart bags and paddling gear.

Duluth Tent & Awing, Inc.
Box 16024, 1610 W. Superior St.
Duluth, MN 55816-0024
(218) 722-3898

Home of the original "Duluth" pack which was designed in 1911 by Camille Porier. These warm and wonderful packs are still made the old fashioned way from the best water-repellent canvas, top grain leather and solid copper rivets. Write for their free catalog which contains dozens of great items.

L.L. Bean, Inc.
Freeport, Maine 04033
1-800-221-4221

Is there anyone who hasn't heard of L.L. Bean? Great store, super catalog and one of the few mail order sources for woven ash pack baskets.

Superior Canoe Packs
PO Box 6687
Minneapolis, MN 55406
(612) 721-5785

Superior Canoe Packs is a division of CLG Enterprises—an internationally known firm that specializes in the manufacture of state-of-the-art outdoor gear. Superior packs feature the finest nickel plated hardware and top grain leather. The company also distributes the excellent *York Pack* (bear resistant plastic wanigan) mentioned in chapter 8.

Camp Trails
P.O. Box 966
Binghamton, NY 13902
(607) 779-2200

A division of Johnson Camping, Camp Trails manufactures state-of-the-art backpacks and accessories.

Stormy Bay Enterprises
P.O. Box 345
Grand Rapids, MN 55744

Manufacturers of the excellent plastic "Wanigan Canoe Pack & Pantry" described in chapter 8.

Joel York & Associates
15 West Main St.
Yarmouth, ME 04096
1-800-348-4923

Manufacturer of the excellent *York Pack* (bear-resistant plastic wanigan) described in chapter 8.

BWCA AND QUETICO CANOEING GUIDE BOOKS

A Paddler's Guide to the Boundary Waters Canoe Area in Northeastern Minnesota, by Michael Duncanson. 76 pp., softcover. Provides detailed descriptions of 31 wilderness canoe routes. Includes 12 updated canoeing maps. Available from W.A. Fisher Company.

Paddlers Guide to Quetico Provincial Park, by Robert Beymer. 168 pages. A guide to 18 entry points and 31 routes. Includes campsite locations, portages, and location of pictographs. Four color fold-out map. Available from W.A. Fisher Company.

Seven Day Menu

See chapter 9 for the specifics of preparing these mouth-watering meals!

DAY	BREAKFAST	LUNCH	SUPPER
1	Canadian bacon, fresh eggs as you like 'em, steamed raisin bagels, Tang™ and coffee	Pita bread, peanut butter and jam (PBJ), hard salami, cookies, instant drink mix	Stir-fry steak, fresh onions, green peppers and tomatoes over rice. Lettuce and tomato salad, Cup-a-Soup
2	Cheese omelet, Canadian bacon, steamed English muffin with margarine and jam. Tang™ and coffee	Pita bread, PBJ, beef jerky, half an apple, salted nut roll, instant drink mix	Smoked bratwursts on the grill, pita bread buns with mustard, Ramen noodle soup
3	Cinnamon-sugar/Rice and golden raisins, stewed mixed evaporated fruit. Tang™ and coffee	Seasoned Rye Krisp, fresh Swiss cheese, carrots, PBJ, "soft batch" chocolate chip cookies, instant drink mix	Hamburger/cheese/vegetable soup with noodles, fresh onion and carrots. Dark chocolate bar (resists melting)
4	Big Bill's Multi Grain Cereal with raisins, dehydrated apples, crushed walnuts and brown sugar. Tang™ and coffee	Pita bread, PBJ, hard salami, mixed nuts, instant drink mix	Spaghetti made with dehydrated hamburger, tomato powder, fresh onion. Cup-a-Soup, M & M's candies
5	Red River Cereal with raisins, dates, crushed walnuts and brown sugar. Tang™ and coffee	Sesame flavored Rye Krisp, fresh Provolone cheese, beef jerky, PBJ, fresh carrots, macaroon cookies, instant drink mix	Pita pizza! Chicken noodle soup. Fresh red cabbage (keeps for days!) and onion salad
6	Multigrain pancakes, fried hard salami, Tang™ and coffee	Pita bread, PBJ, Monterey Jack cheese, GORP, instant drink mix	Chili made with dehydrated hamburger and beans. Add fresh onion and macaroni
7	Cinnamon-sugar tortillas and stewed fruit	Flavored Rye Krisp, fresh dill cheese, PBJ, M & M's peanut candy, instant drink mix	Grilled garlic-cheese pita melt, Ramen noodles with dehydrated hamburger, fresh onion and carrots

The Wilderness Meal

(A Backcountry Ethics Learning Activity)

Please read chapter 5 before doing this activity

Here's a non-intimidating way to teach low impact camping procedures to anyone who is about to experience a Boundary Waters adventure. The activity is structured for Junior High School students, but it has been successfully used—and enthusiastically received—by thousands of adults. It's a natural for schools, scouts, summer camps and nature centers.

You'll need 2-3 hours to prepare students for the activity and pack the food. "Prep time" may be broken into convenient time blocks that suit your schedule. At least 80 minutes of uninterrupted time will be needed for the actual cook-out. Bad weather spoils student attitudes, so reschedule the event if it rains.

OVERVIEW OF THE ACTIVITY

Students build a "no trace" campfire and cook a simple meal that has no bottles or cans to pollute the environment. A "Forest Ranger" (the class instructor) visits the group and quizzes them on the twelve minimum impact rules on their BOUNDARY WATERS WILDERNESS PERMIT (see figure X-1). Students lose points for environmentally incorrect answers and/or not knowing the *rationale* for each rule. After the cook-out, students clean up the fire site and restore the area to pristine condition. The "Ranger" returns, checks for human sign, then awards or deducts points, as necessary.

WHERE TO DO THE ACTIVITY

A wooded setting is best but an outdoor hockey rink, track or graveled school yard works fine. Students "leave no trace" of their activity so there is no damage to the environment. My eighth grade environmental science students have built over 500 fires in a school hockey rink over the last fifteen years, and school administrators can't find one of them!

MATERIALS NEEDED, PER GROUP OF FOUR

1. One three pound coffee can (free from your school cafeteria), fitted with a wire bail made from a coat hanger.
2. Three plastic bags and rubber bands to seal them.
3. A one gallon water container (a clean plastic milk jug is ideal).
4. A sharp pocket knife and small trowel (or substitute an aluminum tube with one end flattened).
5. The instructor furnishes strike anywhere matches.
6. Individual eating utensils—plastic cup, plastic bowl, metal spoon.

UNIT TIMING

Introduction (40 minutes)

1. Begin by telling students that the "Wilderness Meal" activity simulates a real Boundary Waters Experience. Give a brief historical view of the BWCA (see chapter 1) and explain the importance of "low impact" camping. A 21 minute video , Leave No Trace— A Wilderness Ethic, is available at low cost from the BWCA Wilderness Education Consortium (address in appendix 2). Ask your librarian about other films and film strips that teach wilderness ethics.
2. Explain the role of the group leader. The leader is responsible for seeing to it that everyone knows the rules and the rationale behind them. Each group should appoint a "leader."
3. If the activity is done in an unnatural area where firewood cannot be collected, each group must furnish a paper shopping bag filled with dry wood. Wood should range in size from pencil lead thickness to no larger than what can be broken over the knee. Lumber, birch bark, leaves, paper, pine needles and other unnatural materials may not be used!

DISCUSS THE WILDERNESS PERMIT *(40 minutes)*

Hand out *one* copy of the BOUNDARY WATERS WILDERNESS PERMIT (figure X-1) to each group of four people. Read and explain the rationale behind each of the rules. Be prepared for a flood of questions. You may want to review chapters 5, 10 and 12 before you introduce the activity.

DISCUSS LOW-IMPACT FOODS *(40 minutes)*

1. Explain why a "wilderness meal" should be compact, lightweight, waterproof, easy and fast to prepare, and contain no cans or bottles to pollute the environment. Discuss foods which are suitable for a BWCA experience (review chapter 9).
2. The Meal: Groups of 3-4 students will prepare a simple stew from the ingredients listed below.

FOOD ITEMS

- Any favorite instant soup mix. Adjust amounts based on servings per package.
- One cup Bisquick™ or other dumpling mix.
- One cup instant rice.
- Choose any number of these or similar items: Crackers, fruit roll-ups, beef sticks, beef jerky, salted nut rolls, granola bars, GORP (good old raisins and peanuts) made from a mixture of M & M's, Cheerios, sunflower seeds, raisins, peanuts, etc., or candy and cookies that will "melt in your mouth, not in your hands."
- Kool-aid™, Wylers™, Tang™ or other instant flavored drink mix.

FOOD PACKING DAY *(40 minutes)!*

Students follow these guidelines to package their meal

1. Measure one cup of rice into a plastic bag and seal the bag with a rubber band. Set aside this bag.
2. Measure one cup of Bisquick™ into a plastic bag and seal the bag with a rubber band. Set aside this bag.
3. Remove and discard excess packaging on all remaining food items. Pour dry food out of jars into plastic bags.
4. Place all food into a crush-resistant cardboard milk carton and place the carton inside a plastic bag, as illustrated in figure X-2. Non-crushable foods like "Kool-aid" that won't fit may be packed between the milk carton and waterproof plastic bag. Students may use the milk carton to mix powdered soft drinks.

5. Label the milk carton or outer plastic bag with the group leader's name. When students have completed packaging their meal, they should perform these tests:

a) Waterproof test (simulates a canoe capsize): Dunk the meal in a tank of water for 30 seconds.

b) Shock test: Throw the meal lightly(!) against the wall to simulate the abuse of a week on the trail.

6. The instructor keeps all packed meals in a large trash bag for several days prior to the cook-out. This ensures that "illegal" food items that might spoil or melt will!

Figure X-2

Rubber Band –
(if lost it degrades
faster than
plastic twistie)

Milk Carton –
(slit corners of top,
fold over and
seal with tape)

Instant drink mix in packets

Cheese

Crackers

Plastic
bread bag

One Quart
Calibration
mark

Candy Bars

FIRE MAKING DAY *(40-80 minutes)!*

1. (20 minutes) Optional: Read aloud the short story, "To Build A Fire," by Jack London. Prior to reading the tale, challenge students to identify the man's greatest mistake. *Answer:* Instead of building a fire, the man should have brought a change of clothes and a warm sleeping bag. An open fire is not a good survival tool in bitter cold weather.

2. (40-60 minutes) Teach students how to build a "no trace" fire. *Procedure:* Carefully remove a sixteen inch diameter piece of sod with the trowel and set it aside, *upside down.* Then, dig a hole about eight inches deep and pile the diggings on top of the inverted sod cap. Build a hot fire in the hole. Students should whittle fine shavings for tinder and use small twigs for kindling.

   If an outside site is not available to demonstrate fire-building, the instructor should build a mock fire on a table or overhead projector.

3. Students should burn only enough wood to cook the meal. The fire must be allowed to burn until *all* the wood has turned to ashes. The ashes are then doused with water and covered with soil. The sod cap is replaced and the area is smoothed to blend with the environment. No trace of a fire should remain.

COOK-OUT! *(80-100 minutes)*

• Students are assigned "campsites." They dig their holes, light their fires and follow this procedure to cook their meal:

1. Read the directions on the soup package. Add 20 percent more water to the tin can pot than is suggested. Pour the soup mix into the cold water and place the pot on the fire.

2. Add some cold water to the bag of dumpling mix and knead the bag with your hands. Continue to knead and add water until the dough has a soft clay-like consistency. *When the soup in the pot is boiling*, cut a slit in the bag bottom and, using the bag like a cake decorator, force marble sized dumplings into the hot soup.

3. Add the instant rice to the boiling soup.

4. Stir the soup constantly for ten minutes using a long stick whose bark has been removed with a pocket knife.

5. Serve and enjoy!

- At some time during the activity, the instructor (camp ranger) comes on the scene. The ranger asks to see the "Wilderness Permit," then questions students about the rules. Students must know the *rationale* for every regulation. Points are deducted for wrong answers.
- When clean-up is complete, the ranger returns to check each fire-site.

Figure X-1

BOUNDARY WATERS WILDERNESS PERMIT

WELCOME to the Boundary Waters Canoe Area Wilderness! Thousands of people have fought hard to preserve the wilderness character of this region. We hope you will do your part to keep the BWCA clean, green and free of pollution.

You are required to have this permit with you at all times while in the BWCA. You must show your permit to a Forest Ranger on request. Please fill out the information below:

Name of Group Leader _____

Number of Members in the Group _____
(Maximum of *nine* is permitted)

Date _____ **Number of Days You Will Stay** _____
                                in the Boundary Waters

RULES

1. Camp only at designated campsites. Do not occupy just any site.

2. Build fires in designated areas only. Pack out—*do not burn*, aluminum foil! Put your fire *dead out* (check it with your hand) before you leave! A "dead" fire has no visible smoke or steam! Clean up the fire site so as to *leave no trace of humans.*

3. Absolutely no cans or bottles or materials designed to be "obviously disposable" are allowed. This means no styrofoam cups, plastic silverware or margarine tubs!

4. Use only dead and downed wood for fire building. Go far away from the lakeshore and your campsite to collect firewood.

5. Cutting or marking living trees is strictly prohibited! Do not peel birch bark or remove leaves or branches from living trees.

6. Do not dig a trench around your tent to carry away storm water. Trenching is ugly and it causes serious soil erosion. You'll stay dry in rain if you place a plastic groundcloth *inside* your tent.

7. Burn your trash, and *pack out* what won't burn! Be sure you have brought a strong plastic trash bag for this purpose. Hang your trash bag from a tree limb so you can find it easily. Forest Rangers may ask to see your trash bag!

8. *Be aware of your campsite responsibility.* You are *required* to keep a clean, orderly campsite *at all times.* If you generate trash, pick it up immediately and put it in your trash bag. If your campsite was trashed by thoughtless persons before you, *you* must clean up their mess!

9. Do not wash dishes, bathe or swim within 150 feet from a lake or river. Dishes—and your body—should be washed (with biodegradable soap) and rinsed on land, well away from open water.

10. If nature calls and no official latrine (toilet) is available, go out of the camp area, 150 feet from water, and carefully bury human waste and toilet paper under a 4-6 inch cover of soil.

11. Respect the rights of others! Loud screaming, radios and other disturbing sounds will not be tolerated.

12. Leave your campsite in a natural state. *Do not* lash or nail logs together to make tables, chairs or other furniture. These activities spoil the wilderness experience for the next party who will occupy your campsite.

MAP INDEX

BWCAW QUETICO

A1. BWCA and Quetico Area Map
A1. - Laminated
1. Pine, Greenwood, Mountain
2. E. Bearskin, Clearwater, Alder
3. Ball Club, Winchell, Poplar
4. Gunflint, Loon, North
4A. Gunflint W/ Water Depths
5. Magnetic, Gunflint, Northern L.
6. Saganga, Sea Gull
6A. Saganga, Saganagons
7. Little Saganaga, Tuscarora
8. Knife, Kekekabic, Thomas
9. Moose, Basswood, Snowbank
10. Basswood, Crooked, Sarah
10A. Basswood Depth Contour Map
11. Jackfish, Beartrap, Thursday
12. Moose River, Stuart
13. Lac La Croix
14. Loon, Wilkins, Little Indian Sioux
15. Trout
16. Burntside, Cummings
17. Fall, Pipestone
18. Lake One, Bald Eagle
19. Isabella, Insula
20. Alton, Perent
21. Sawbill, Brule, Pipe
22. Arrow, Sandstone
23. Iron Range, Canthook, Jinx
24. Northern Light
25. Saganagons, Mack
26. This Man, Cache
27. Agnes, Kahshahpiwi
28. Brent, Poobah, Conmee
29. Argo, Minn, William
30. Red Pine, Badwater, Snow
31. Lac La Croix, Wolsely, Nam.R.
32. Thompson, David, Namakan R.
33. Beaverhouse, Whalen, Factor
34. Quetico, Cirrus, McCauly
35. Sturgeon, Burntside, Jean
36. Keefer, Williams, Camel
37. Kawnipi

BWCAW QUETICO

38. Powell, Obadinaw R. Wawiag R.
39. Titmarsh, Plummens, Nelson
40. Burchell
41. Tilly, Windigoostigwan
42. McKenzie, Cache, Buckingham
43. Russel, Olifaunt, Maligne R.
44. Soho, Kasakokwog, Oriana
45. Pickerel, Batchewaung, Nym
46. Pickerel, Eva, Baptism
116. Ely, Shagawa

VOYAGEURS NATIONAL PARK

K1. Kabetogama
N1. Namakan, Sand Point
C1. Crane, Sand Point
R1. Rainy Lake Southwest
R2. Rainy Lake Southeast

ISLE ROYALE

IRE. Isle Royale East
IRC. Isle Royale Central
IRW. Isle Royale West

LAKE SUPERIOR

AI . Apostle Is.
CA. Chequamegon Bay/Apostle.Is.
DS. Duluth/Superior
PC. Port Wing /Cornucopia
TS. Two Harbors/ Silver Bay

MN. NORTH SHORE AREA
SUPERIOR NAT'L FOREST

98. Grand Portage
99. Tom Lake
100. Grand Marais
101. Cascade- Bally Creek
102. Lutsen-Tofte
103. Taconite Harbor -Little Marais
104. Beaver Bay- Tettegouche
105. Gooseberry
203. Timber- Frear
204. Dumbell Lake
304. Silver Island

General Map Information

MCKENZIE MAPS of the BWCAW and QUETICO
PROVINCIAL PARK are published on a scale of
2" = 1mile. Each map covers an area of
approximately 144 square miles. The maps are
printed on a 25" x 30" sheet of POLYART plastic
paper which is next to indestructible. They are
totally waterproof and extremely hard to tear even
after folding many times. The maps will easily
withstand all the hard use you can give them. They
even float!

MCKENZIE MAPS can be used for
navigation. They contain the most up-to-date
information on campsite locations, portages,
hiking trails, ski trails, motor regulations,
navigation markers where used, topography, and
hydrographics.

In addition to a single 25" x 38" souvenir or
planning map that covers all of the BWCAW and
90% of QUETICO PARK, there are 25 maps of the
BWCAW and 25 QUETICO maps. All maps are
reviewed for accuracy by Park officials, U.S.
Forest Service officials, DNR officials, guides,
outfitters, and resort owners.

Sizes of the other maps vary. There five 25" x 38"
maps of VOYAGEURS NATIONAL PARK, three
25" x 38" maps of ISLE ROYALE, five 25" x 38"
maps of LAKE SUPERIOR and APOSTLE IS.
NATIONAL LAKESHORE and eleven 25" x 30" or
25" x 38" maps of the Minnesota North Shore of
Lake Superior and Superior National Forest. The
North Shore maps show the most recent
information on Minnesota's popular SUPERIOR
HIKING TRAIL.

MCKENZIE MAPS can be purchased at most
sporting goods stores, resorts, outfitters, park
offices or by calling or writing MCKENZIE
PRODUCTS, 315 W. Michigan St., Duluth, MN.
55802, 218-727-2113.

A special thanks to Rod McKenzie for
allowing me to use this McKenzie Map
index.

The circled number close to the center of each map indicates the map border you desire.

Boundary Waters Canoe Area Wilderness,
Quetico Provincial Park and
Voyageurs National Park

MAPS
BY
McKENZIE

DISTRIBUTED BY McKENZIE
PRODUCTS

1
2
3
4

"feather"
the paddle
back through
the water

UNDERWATER STROKE
Use this quiet stroke for approaching wildlife.

PITCH STROKE

Wrist bends
inward

PADDLE BLADE LEGEND
O = Outside (power) face
I = Inside face

Outside (power) face   Inside face

PITCH STROKE
An effective traveling stroke.